The Computer Networking Book

The Computer Networking Book

Peter O'Dell

VENTANA PRESS

The Computer Networking Book
Copyright © 1989 by Peter O'Dell

Library of Congress Cataloging-in-Publication Data

O'Dell, Peter, 1956-
    The computer networking book/by Peter O'Dell.—1st ed.
      p. cm.
    ISBN 0-940087-38-3 :
    1. Computer networks. I. Title.
TK5105.5.032 1989
650'.028'546—dc20   89-38426

Book design: Karen Wysocki, Ventana Press
Cover design: Dancing Bear Graphics, Raleigh, NC
Cover photography: Steve Muir, Henderson-Muir Photography, Raleigh, NC
Illustrations: Keith Cassell, Cassell Design, Durham, NC
Typesetting: Pixel Plus Desktop Publishing, Chapel Hill, NC
Editor: Marion Laird
Editorial Staff: Elizabeth Shoemaker, Terry Patrickis

First Edition, Second Printing
Printed in the United States of America

Ventana Press, Inc.
P.O. Box 2468
Chapel Hill, NC 27515
919/942-0220
FAX 919/942-1140

Limits of Liability and Disclaimer of Warranty

About The Author

Peter O'Dell is manager of Information Services at Autodesk, Inc. of Sausalito, California, and has previously worked at DEC, Criton Technologies and Microsoft. He has written articles for various magazines on the subjects of strategic planning, prototyping, MRP and user-developed systems. He may be reached at

8 Creek Side Way
Mill Valley, CA 94941

or via MCI Mail:

Peter ODell/Sausalito
MCI ID: 365-0583

Dedication

To my wife, Lisa. Thanks for your unwavering support and encouragement with this book and everything else I've done.

Acknowledgments

Thanks to the entire Management Information Systems Department at Autodesk. I've never worked with a better group of individuals.

Neil Evans of Microsoft, Perry Cole of DEC, and Jim James of Vanguard Technology provided valuable (and tactful) feedback on the content.

Trademarks

Trademarked names appear throughout this book. Rather than list the names and entities that own the trademarks or insert a trademark symbol with each mention of the trademarked name, the publisher states that it is using the names only for editorial purposes and to the benefit of the trademark owner with no intention of infringing upon that trademark.

Contents

Introduction

Why a "Plain-English" Networking Book?

The personal computer has brought major changes to American business. Never has the power to manipulate and share large quantities of information been so widespread and inexpensive. Sharing information (networking) among these millions of computers is the new technological hurdle organizations are now facing. In fact, networks are now being implemented at the same rate at which personal computers were being installed in the early to mid-1980s.

Until now, key decisions about how to initiate and use the technology have remained in the hands of a relative few. Most books associated with computer networks have addressed the gurus, the technical "inner circle." Management and the uninitiated have been kept in the dark and have been virtually uninvolved in decisions, due to a lack of understanding and the inability to tie business goals to a technical solution.

The Computer Networking Book was written to help nontechnical managers make important decisions about how and when to link up their computers. It explores, in "plain English," the entire range of strategies and technologies; from simple, inexpensive "try-me" scenarios to full-blown solutions that can last for many years.

When you finish this book, you'll know enough to talk intelligently with your technical peers, including consultants and vendors. And you'll realize you don't need a degree in computer science to make an informed decision.

Who Should Read This Book?

If you're one of the millions of business owners or managers who have two or more personal computers and are trying to figure out the best way to link them together, *The Computer Networking Book* will be of value to you and your company. There's no question that a well-implemented program for sharing computer information can enhance productivity and cut costs.

Making the right decisions about computer networking is like making other business decisions: you need to consider your company's goals, growth rate, cash flow and many other nontechnical issues. *The Computer Networking Book* is the only guide that addresses networking issues from the perspective of a business person, in terms of management considerations that should drive your decisions in the first place.

What's Inside

The book is organized into three parts:

Chapters 1 through 6 help you determine whether you need to share computer information, including a number of solutions. Sometimes, your company just needs to change its *systems* without investing in expensive technologies. And often a simple, low-cost networking alternative is best, and can save your company cash and headaches.

Chapters 7 through 10 explore the more complex "local area networks," the most popular long-term solution. You'll learn the basics of evaluating alternatives, designing and implementing your solution and keeping it operational.

Included in several chapters you'll find real-world examples, outlines and checklists to apply to your own business operations.

Chapter 11 features some advanced technologies available now, as well as future network capabilities that will be available soon. Planning for them can save money and give you a strategic advantage.

How Much Do You Need to Know?

If you have a basic understanding of computers and how they're used within your company, you'll be able to understand this book. Acquiring and implementing a means for sharing information among your computers aren't any harder than making other complex business decisions once you understand the critical components. The information provided here will demystify these elements and provide an intelligent roadmap for action.

This book doesn't try to encompass the entire body of knowledge about information-sharing and computer networks (that would require a 5,000-page book that would be out of date before it was finished). What we address here are the fundamentals of understanding, choosing, implementing and managing a computer network—not by a high-paid professional but by "ordinary people" who must incorporate this powerful set of tools to accomplish real work.

There is no one perfect solution for all businesses. Every organization looking at sharing computer information will have different requirements, ranging from the need to share files and printers across two desks to a multinational computer network comprising hundreds of disparate machines. There are, however, universal common-sense guidelines that can be applied by the person responsible for supervising the operation of these functions. *The Computer Networking Book* will help you put computers and sharing information into a proper nontechnical perspective so that you can effectively communicate—and delegate—your company's networking needs.

One word of advice: check the published date of this book before investing a lot of time reading it. If it's more than two years old, get an updated copy or find a new book. What might be great advice in 1989 will be history by 1992. Computers are more sophisticated, more interconnected, faster, cheaper, more reliable and easier to use than ever, a trend which will accelerate sharply over the next several years, especially in the area of networks and connectivity.

I hope this book convinces you that your computers are a strategic resource that can be understood and managed much like the company car or company telephone system. You may not know all the answers, but you can determine what you need and how much it's worth to you. Let's get started.

Peter O'Dell
Mill Valley, CA

Networking Questions and Answers

Do you remember when you left the typewriter and adding machine stage behind, stepped into the brave new world of electronics and purchased your first computer equipment? You had to learn new concepts and a battery of foreign terminology. It probably took some time for you and your co-workers to feel comfortable and in control of the new equipment.

Now it seems hard to remember the old ways of processing information, and conversing in the new vocabulary of computerese has become familiar and natural.

If the term 'computer networking' evokes old anxieties and seems complex and intimidating, it shouldn't. Networking computers means joining them together with wiring and software for enhanced communication, convenience and efficiency.

To introduce you to networking, I've selected the most frequently asked questions from the workshops and seminars I've conducted, and some that have evolved from my case studies of companies involved in a networking project or considering which way to go.

The concise question-and-answer format gives you an overview of the basic issues involved in connecting personal computers. These issues are covered more thoroughly in succeeding chapters.

What is a computer network?

A computer network can best be defined as two or more computers connected to each other via electronic means for the purpose of exchanging information (word processing files, accounting database information, electronic mail or customer records) or sharing common computer equipment, such as an expensive laser printer or plotter.

Networks can be small (two personal computers sharing a printer) or large (thousands of computers of all sizes and types). They can be local (within an office or company), national or international. They can be private (owned by a single company such as General Motors or Bill's Bike Shop) or public (available for use by many companies or individuals, such as Tymnet). They can be as simple as a single cable running from one PC to another, or complex, using satellites, microwaves, fiber optics and special telephone circuits.

Whether the system is simple or sophisticated, the common purpose of computer networking is to exchange information faster and easier than if the machines weren't networked, and to lay the groundwork for enhanced applications and communications between users.

How do computers share information?

Computers can share information in a number of ways, each with its own advantages and costs:

Floppy Disks: Floppies can be copied from one computer to another in order to update information (sometimes known as "sneaker-net," after the footwear used to carry the information between computers).

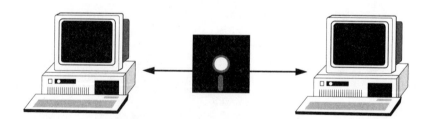

Figure 1.1   Sneaker-net: the low-tech solution.

Computer Tapes: Usually in cartridge form, these tapes can be used to distribute information among computers. For example, a company's main customer file may reside in the accounting computer. During the day, any changes that occur are made to that copy of the file. Each night, the customer file is copied to the tape, which is then manually copied to other computers.

PC-to-PC Connection: Information can be copied from one personal computer to another, using a connecting cable along with software installed on each PC.

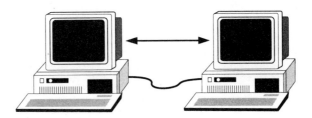

Figure 1.2   Matchmakers: PC-to-PC connection.

Host System: A PC may be connected to a large, central computer by cable or telephone line, with information "downloaded" for local use. Information from another PC could be "uploaded" for later transfer to other personal computers.

Personal Computer Network: A number of computers are linked together with software, hardware and cables, allowing people to share information concurrently with others on the network, rather than having separate working copies of the information.

How do I know if I need to share information among my computers?

If you need to be more productive within your organization, sharing information between your computers can help. Indications of the need for greater information-sharing include

Duplicate Processing: Entering of invoices or inventory information by several people into different systems within the company.

Duplicate Information: For example, having multiple copies of the same information on different computers can produce conflicting information and require additional maintenance time.

Waiting for Equipment: If people are queuing up to use a certain printer because they can't access it from their computer, valuable time is wasted.

Manual Processing: One or more employees devoting a lot of time to maintaining manual logs of information and distributing copies.

Delays and Errors: Organizational disruption surrounding a particular event, such as reconciling inventory each month or printing a consolidated set of customer labels.

Misunderstandings: If verbal instructions are constantly interpreted incorrectly, they may be too complex. Having a system for sharing information can help alleviate this problem.

What you need may be as simple as exchanging floppies or having a common tape drive among your computers. If your needs are more complex, you may need to consider a local area network (LAN), (described later in this chapter) for your organization.

How can networking enhance productivity?

The major purpose of installing computers in an organization is to enhance productivity—avoiding extra work and raising the accuracy level. Having access to common information from several computers is an effective way of accomplishing this objective. This is the reason for the explosion of networking in recent years.

As a simple example of the need to share common information, let's say that Jerry's Welding Shop has two personal computers—one in accounting and one on the shipping dock—that aren't connected to each other in any way. Changes to addresses are made through word of mouth and scribbled notes between departments (forms were made up for this once, but they got lost during a reorganization).

Jerry receives an emergency order from one of his best customers, who has just moved from New York to San Francisco. Jerry processes the order in the accounting computer, changing the address of the customer for billing information. The order is then sent to the shop. Barbara, the shop manager, fills the order as specified, and sends the material to shipping. Sam in shipping prepares the shipping paper work using the old address, since he doesn't know the customer has moved. The shipping paper work is printed out with the wrong address and the material is sent off to New York instead of San Francisco.

The customer is enraged and Jerry's Welding has needlessly created customer service problems and incurred extra expense. If only the two computers could have shared the customer information, Jerry, Sam and Barbara wouldn't have to meet at the unemployment office each week!

Does every organization need a network?

Not necessarily, at least not now. In the future, voice and data communications will be so interrelated that an organization will be required to integrate them in order to survive. How many businesses do you know that don't provide a telephone for almost every employee? New functions such as electronic mail (both internal and external) and the use of outside database information will cause many organizations to connect their internal network to outside networks. Network use will outstrip telephone use within some organizations, and, perhaps sooner than you think, the phone and the computer will be merged into one single communications device.

Business is getting more time-competitive, and technology that is applied judiciously can make a big difference in terms of quality and timeliness. The type of network needed can vary widely from business to business. Don't feel that you need the most expensive network available—if you buy a system you can't fully use, you may negate the benefits you achieve. This book shows you how to focus on the appropriate solution rather than the most expensive one.

What do most businesses or organizations need?

It has been estimated that between 70 and 80 percent of business communications are local, within the confines of an office or factory. A system known as a local area network (LAN) is used to connect computers located within a few kilometers of each other, typically with privately owned cable or wiring. This type of network allows sharing information and devices cost-effectively and at very high speeds. A variety of computers can be attached, giving the organization a way to connect diverse "islands of automation" that may have already sprung up.

LANs are a fairly recent technical innovation. In 1987, only 10 percent of personal computers were connected to networks; by 1992, it's estimated that 55 to 65 percent of personal computers will be connected to LANs.

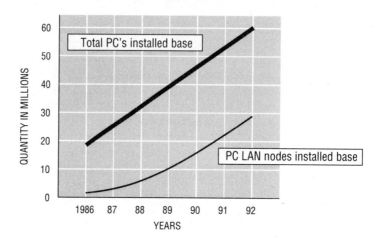

Figure 1.3   **Here today, everywhere tomorrow:
PC LAN growth projections.**
Source: International Data Corp. 1988.

A LAN can be connected to other local area networks as well, to form
the basis for effective information-sharing between departments and
organizations. LANs can be made up of all small computers or a mixture of large and small computers. Through interconnecting LANs
among companies, electronic mail is replacing conventional paper
work. Because of their flexibility and capabilities, PC LANs are the
primary focus of this book.

What advantages will a LAN give me?

Sharing information is the biggest single benefit; sharing expensive
peripherals on the network runs a close second. Without a network,
information must be exchanged by physically printing out results or
by producing a floppy disk. The capability for transparently sharing
expensive computer peripherals (such as a high-speed laser printer
or color plotter) assures full utilization of those resources, avoids the
costs of buying additional hardware, and gives everyone access from
his or her own computer.

Networked applications software (e.g., an accounts payable package)
allows several users access to the same information without maintaining separate copies on each PC. Enhanced integration of many

functions can be accomplished—for example, the PC used in shipping can instantly query credit information to ensure that credit limits aren't exceeded. If your organization has a minicomputer or mainframe, some applications can be offloaded to the LAN, avoiding or postponing expensive capacity upgrades to the large machine.

How would a typical LAN work?

Let's say your organization is an architectural firm that comprises ten employees—seven architects and three administrative assistants. Each person has a PC (the architects might have high-speed computers to handle the complicated calculations associated with developing complex drawings). The architects use a computer-aided design software package that allows them to develop high-quality architectural drawings much faster than they could by manual drafting board methods. The support people do accounting, quoting/estimating of new projects and word processing.

Each PC is connected to the LAN with a network interface card installed inside each computer. There's also some network software set up in each computer's memory that is activated when the unit is turned on. The LAN is made up of a cable that links all the individual PCs to a dedicated PC (with a large-capacity hard-disk storage unit) called a *network file server*. The server has special software that coordinates the exchange of information between each of the other PCs, as well as acting as the common storage area. Also attached to the server is a high-speed plotter that can be used by all the architects to plot their preliminary and final drawings. Also, the network can provide all the PCs with access to the same laser printer, avoiding the costs of buying a printer for each person.

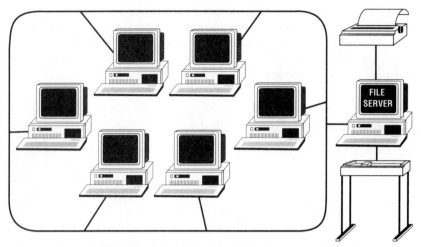

Figure 1.4   Full-blown LAN with file-server nucleus.

Everyone on the network can exchange E-mail, instead of tediously writing out messages in longhand. With a modem and some software attached to the network file server, all employees can access vendors and customers via MCI Mail and other systems even if the customer doesn't have a computer. This service provides access by electronic mail, fax or printed letters—all from the user's PC, with no paper produced.

Using multi-user project management and bill-of-materials software, the estimator, architect and accountant can access information about the same project at the same time, since it's stored on the server. Project information can be transferred to a local spreadsheet for further analysis.

With a modem and communications software installed on your network, remote access is also possible. For example, via lap-top computer and modem, an architect traveling in a distant city can access the file server to send back changes to a project for further cost analysis.

Are there other types of networks?

Yes. You may have read about something called a wide area network (WAN). In a WAN, the "nodes" (individual computers that make up the network) are widely separated. The distance between them may be several miles or thousands of miles. A WAN may be made up of several LANs or a LAN and a remote "host" (usually a large-scale computer—a mainframe or minicomputer—that can handle many tasks and many users at the same time).

Large networks within large companies facilitate communications around the world. For example, many large corporations have a global network that allows employees to communicate with each other around the world and around the clock. One software engineer in Massachusetts recently used his colleague's computers in Australia while everyone there was asleep!

Why is a PC LAN better than a minicomputer with several terminals?

Regrettably, there is no hard-and-fast rule, and the number of viable solutions is growing larger rather than smaller. For an organization with stand-alone PCs only, a LAN allows the continued use of existing PCs and software already familiar and operational, so the impact on the organization is usually minimized.

In general, a LAN can be built in small steps, while a minicomputer involves a single, large capital outlay and implementation to make it work. LAN software is less expensive on the whole. If one PC on the network breaks, the rest of the network can continue to function. If the minicomputer breaks, everything stops until it's fixed.

There's also the question of obsolescence—a LAN can be upgraded one piece at a time, spreading costs over a longer period of time. The minicomputer is usually replaced in whole, although innovative minicomputer vendors have implemented upgrades that involve a simple replacement of circuit boards for additional power and features. In the past, minicomputer vendors have typically provided better support, training and ongoing maintenance. However, PC networking companies are rapidly closing the gap.

If this sounds terribly confusing, think about the type of vehicle you might buy for your organization. If you operate a quarry, you probably need a large truck (or several), along with special digging equipment. If you run an inner-city delivery service, you might need a fleet of bicycles. A large pizza chain may need a delivery fleet of vehicles that are small and easy to maintain, but may also need a large truck for delivery of supplies. Is there one right answer for all of these companies? No. And the same is true for computer systems—

the solution depends on the unique requirements of your organization. (You'll learn the trade-offs between the basic alternatives in Chapter 4.)

Because of the increased competition between LANs and minicomputers, the winners will be the consumers, who will have a variety of good options to choose from.

If I want to install a network, do I have to do it all at one time?

No. In fact your chances of succeeding are enhanced by *not* rushing into things. What's important is developing an information-sharing plan based on the expectations for your business or organization (see Chapter 3). Once your plan is in place, you can begin to implement items *one step at a time*, starting with the highest-payoff project first. That way, if you need to stop or slow down, you've accomplished the most important goals.

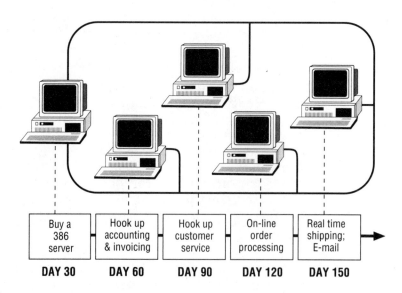

Buy a 386 server	Hook up accounting & invoicing	Hook up customer service	On-line order processing	Real time shipping; E-mail
DAY 30	**DAY 60**	**DAY 90**	**DAY 120**	**DAY 150**

Figure 1.5   Network layaway plan: linking up in stages.

Another benefit of addressing these critical functions first is that you can start realizing payoffs quickly, which will help to offset any outlay of capital for necessary investments. Secondary tasks can be evaluated at a point when the most critical issues have been solved and are producing benefits for the organization.

How much does a network cost?

The cost of a network can vary widely depending on the computers attached and the tasks to be accomplished. A simple network that allows several PCs to exchange information and share devices can be constructed for a few dollars per computer. Fully functional networks can cost as much as thousands of dollars per computer.

For an approximate figure, an average PC network costs between $2,000 and $5,000 per PC in hardware and software costs, including the interface cards, cable, file server and network software. This can vary widely, depending on the company's needs.

It's up to management to decide what's needed. If the goals for the network are well defined and the implementation fits those goals, the odds are high that it will quickly pay for itself through cost efficiency or enhanced productivity. Like most other areas of technology, the cost of networking has decreased rather dramatically, and this trend should continue.

Can I use my existing PCs?

If you're using IBM or IBM-compatible personal computers, almost all of them—as well as Macintosh, 32-bit workstations and others—can be attached to a personal computer network in one way or another. (Machines from Atari and older Apple computers usually do not work on a PC network.)

In almost all cases, a LAN will help extend the useful life of the equipment you're already using. By attaching older equipment to a network, newer network resources—such as increased disk storage—can be accessed. This affords users of older or obsolete equipment enhanced performance and a wider range of resources without constantly adding the latest innovations, more memory and other capabilities to the machine. This is one of the strongest incentives for using a PC network: equipment can be added a piece at a time rather than in large, expensive upgrades.

What about existing and new software?

Your existing PC software can run unchanged in most cases, again preserving your investment. In addition, network versions of most popular software are available at a cost per user that's substantially lower than the cost of individual copies. When new versions are released, only the network version needs to be updated, so that translations take less time, and overall management control is increased.

Installing a network will also give your organization the capability to use software that cannot be used on a stand-alone PC. Software such as electronic mail and calendaring systems, which are aimed at raising the productivity of a department or larger work group, can be implemented once a LAN is in place. (Chapter 6 focuses on the multi-user and the issues and benefits of standardizing application software on your network.)

Our company has a mainframe—can a LAN connect to it?

In most cases a LAN can connect to an existing minicomputer or mainframe system using special software and/or hardware known as a *gateway* (discussed in Chapter 8). The gateway allows the LAN and the host system to exchange data and share devices such as high-speed printers.

Many larger companies are beginning to decentralize information rather than keeping it locked up in the corporate computer room. This increased access expedites the flow of information among the various divisions or departments of the company, and allows some tasks previously done on the corporate mainframe to be done more easily, inexpensively and effectively on PCs.

Spreadsheets and interactive graphics are examples of these tasks. Although spreadsheet programs are available on mainframes and minicomputers, most people choose to run them on PCs because of the simplicity and the "cheap" computer or processing cycles available on PCs. Many products have become available to assist in making these connections, allowing data to be shared in batches and on a continual basis. For example, sales information for the prior month might be downloaded to a PC in the marketing department, where market forecasts can be developed using several different spreadsheet models. The final projections can be uploaded to the mainframe inventory program and used as the basis for ordering components.

Our organization has Macintosh computers and PCs—can they communicate over a LAN?

Yes, many major network vendors offer special programs that allow Apple's Macintosh computers to exchange information and share peripherals with IBM-compatible PCs. It seems certain that the communication functions between PCs and the Macintosh will continue to improve.

Many software companies provide a common data file format that allows PC and Macintosh versions to work with the same information without translation (AutoCAD and Microsoft Excel are two good examples). This high level of integration will continue to develop over the next several years, allowing increased interaction among various types of computers.

In the not-too-distant future, it will be possible to transparently mix all types of computers on a single network, allowing users to purchase the best equipment for a particular task without worrying about compatibility.

Where can I get a network?

You can get the components for a network from the same sources you would use to purchase computer equipment. Solutions range from do-it-yourself kits, available through computer magazines, to multibillion-dollar companies that will come into your organization and install everything for you (just sign on the dotted line and write the check!). Networking became a billion-dollar business in 1987 and promises to grow at a fast rate (30 percent-plus) for the next ten years. Many computer dealers are setting up special departments and hiring personnel to sell, install and maintain PC networks.

Prospective buyers should be wary, however. In the past, there was always someone who had a brother-in-law in real estate or used cars that could get you a great "deal." Now that same person is in the computer consulting business and can get you a great deal on a small network that was used only once a month by its former owners. The vendors you deal with for your solutions are critical to your success. In Chapter 9, you'll learn to evaluate them carefully and to ensure that your best interests are served.

Another caution: don't allow yourself to fall into a solution. By letting a solution emerge rather than planning it, you can end up with a mess. If you simply allow a network to happen, it will cost you money and create many long-term problems.

How do I decide what I need?

Deciding when to install a network and which type to install is much like making any other business equipment decision. Analyze what you want to accomplish, how much you want to spend and when you need it, keeping in mind what your organization can absorb financially and functionally. This book outlines many of the issues involved in evaluating your networking needs and the effort involved in getting your system working.

The key to a successful implementation is to be well informed—not with a lot of technical details but with a basic understanding of the underlying principles of networking and how it will help your organization achieve its business goals. Managers can delegate the work but not the responsibility on this particular task; wrong decisions at early stages will have far-reaching consequences that can affect the entire organization.

I read something about "open systems" recently. Does this affect my buying decision?

It could. Open systems is the overall concept of multiple vendors' hardware and software working together without proprietary boundaries. If you think of a stereo made up of various components and apply it to computer systems, you'll get a clear picture. Previously (and still the case with some vendors), only the vendor's peripheral equipment would work with the vendor's computer. Software was designed to run only on the vendor's proprietary operating system, locking the customer into a vendor regardless of their performance. Open systems (based mostly around Unix, MS-DOS and OS/2) promise the user a better and more connected world. This affects networking as well, allowing more computers to talk to each other as open systems initiatives take effect. The full impact of this movement won't be felt for at least a few more years, but it will have a major effect on the computer industry.

Wouldn't it be easier to get one of the huge computer companies to do the whole job?

This is certainly one viable alternative available to you, but it isn't that simple. (If it were, there wouldn't be so many small vendors growing so fast.) Most large computer companies are oriented toward large-scale solutions and may not be interested in small installations. Also, the major vendors tend to bid all of their own equipment, which can limit the functionality of a LAN (and raise your costs).

Get proposals from several vendors and decide which one seems the most interested in and capable of helping you achieve your business goals within your price range (see Chapter 9).

Can I avoid having large, unsightly computer cables?

Yes. Cabling for computer networks has improved tremendously over the last few years. Recent technology will allow you to run high-speed networks using normal telephone wiring, which is probably already installed in your building. Other networks also utilize this type of wiring, allowing for a very clean installation.

The more mature technology available today minimizes the cabling breakdowns that were common in early networks. With recent innovations to cabling and other network equipment, the reliability of networks has been greatly increased.

Will I need a full-time programmer or technical person to maintain the network?

Not in most cases. Network hardware and software are becoming easier to install and use, and people within organizations are becoming more computer-literate. Many organizations appoint one person to take care of the network on a part-time basis, or several people to share the responsibilities involved. Outside services can also be obtained for assistance. To avoid problems as your dependence on your network increases, the level of commitment and resources should also increase.

Apply the same logic for allocating resources to cover technical personnel that you'd apply to any other business decision. For example, if you were a precious-metals dealer, you would probably invest more time and money in a security system and vault than a gas station would. The same applies to technology. Spend more time and money on the components you depend upon for successful operation to ensure that they're stable, protected, in top operating condition and well managed.

What do I do when equipment breaks down?

Several options are available. You can hire employees who have sufficient expertise to handle almost all problems, though this can be an expensive proposition. Service contracts available from major vendors or dealers can guarantee a certain level of service. Many organizations opt for a contract based on time and materials: when something goes wrong, the servicing company's charges for the repair work are based on an agreed-upon hourly rate plus the cost of the materials necessary to make the repairs. (Chapter 10 addresses ways of keeping your network operational once it's installed.)

Computer equipment has become much more reliable over the last few years, which allows for some risk-taking. I have had some equipment become obsolete long before it broke down, even when it was running 24 hours a day. With prices decreasing, having redundant equipment can be cheaper than paying 10 to 20 percent of the list price for a service contract.

If you have a multimillion-dollar business that relies on the accuracy of your computer customer file, don't scrimp on the resources necessary to ensure success. On the other hand, if a broken computer is a minor inconvenience to your company, don't spend thousands of dollars maintaining nonessential equipment.

Again comparing computer technology to other common business problems, these are the same choices you face when buying a company vehicle, and the same rules apply. Match the solution with the importance level. If you can do without a particular piece of equipment for several days, you might be able to repair it when it breaks. But if it's a vital piece of your business, you need to have a plan in place for immediate maintenance or backup equipment.

I know people who've tried to network their computers and aren't happy with the results. How can I succeed where others have failed?

Several factors are on your side—time and technical advances. Networking technology is reaching the public mainstream; it's becoming easier to use and to understand, more standardized and less expensive.

Also research your options thoroughly before acting. Knowledge is the best cure for the fear and frustration of the unknown. Do your homework. Read this book and others before investing in the equipment and time necessary to network your computers. Seminars and site visits will also help.

With most computer projects, the time to catch mistakes is early on. As time goes by, the cost of fixing a mistake rises steeply. Planning will help catch at least the large mistakes while it's still inexpensive to fix them (see Chapter 3).

Talk to your friends or associates who failed or achieved less than desired results. Find out where they went wrong, what they would have done differently if only they had known what they know now. Talk to people who've successfully done what you want to do within a similar budget. If you cannot find anyone who has, you may be setting unrealistic expectations; in terms of payoff, only the most strategic projects warrant doing something that has never been done.

What about obsolescence? I don't want to start over in a few months!

Obsolete equipment is a genuine worry for all organizations, especially in the rapidly changing computer industry. By purchasing quality products that are current standards or are becoming standards, an organization will have the best chance of obtaining a long life from systems equipment. And manufacturers are providing upgrades to many pieces of equipment, in response to an ever-increasing base of users who want to upgrade rather than replace.

A network can actually help to prolong the life of equipment, because a faster and more capable system can provide a path for older equipment over the network.

What will happen if I wait?

Waiting for better solutions has its pros and cons. If you wait, you avoid the capital outlays, installation and operations involved with a new strategy. You'll probably also save, because the price/performance curve on equipment has continued downward, offering more power and capability for less money.

But there are problems with waiting as well. If the pain and frustration levels within your company are already high, start looking at solutions now. If the critical functions you want to computerize are already past the point where they need automation, waiting will only aggravate the problems. There's always a learning period with new technology, and pushing that into the unknown future is a risk in itself. What happens if you get a big increase in business and need to automate while that growth spurt is in full tilt?

Moving On

If you get the sense that planning and setting business goals make all the difference, go to the head of the class. Merely jumping into a network and delegating its installation and operation away from top management's attention will certainly cause your organization to spend more money and realize fewer benefits. Who is better equipped than a company's executives to set strategic direction for this vital function?

Ultimately, management has to live with the decisions that are made. If you're in a decision-making position, plan carefully; you'll be purchasing and installing a useful system that will last many years if the right decisions are made.

Another major point I want to get across to everyone involved in choosing a solution is not to get confused or overwhelmed by the technology. Some decisions relate to the technology but are secondary to the main goal of any computer-based project—to enhance the profitability and effectiveness of an organization. The technology must always be secondary to this goal, and decision-makers should focus relentlessly on the business goals.

Insist on having technical items explained in *your* language. You're writing the check; you deserve this courtesy. Ask questions—no matter how simplistic they sound. ROI (return on investment) may be second nature to you, but when someone starts talking about network protocol stacks, there's nothing wrong with asking for an English translation and an explanation of how they relate to your overall business goals. Make vendors explain how their proposals can affect your business, and what the alternatives are. If a solution can't be stated in terms of the organization's goals, you have every right to question the technology or the sales pitch.

In the next chapter, you'll look at the specifics of how sharing computer information can deliver benefits to your organization. You'll also begin to focus on the activities within your organization that might return the highest networking payoffs.

What Will a Network Buy My Organization?

Costs and benefits are among the first issues that come up when you're considering sharing information and hooking up computers. Many businesses take a dim view of the benefits that technology offers, and with good reason. Many past solutions, that were touted as "breakthroughs" and "innovative," have caused organizations to spend money on unneeded or low-priority projects that didn't fulfill their promises of improving the bottom line. In this chapter, we look at substantial benefits that a network solution can provide, and show you how to make it work within your budget.

While reviewing these benefits, look at your own organization with a critical eye. It does little good to list benefits of a solution if you don't believe they're achievable or worth striving for. Any solution that involves technology also requires commitment; merely doing something because someone else recommends it is a poor way to approach making anything successful.

Where to Aim: Mission-Critical Systems

Here come the technical buzzwords, right? Not really. The mission-critical systems are those systems or functions within your organization that ultimately spell the difference between success and failure. Consider the following examples:

For a *hospital*, patient care would take precedence over supplies inventory (I certainly hope so, anyway). Having the right supplies in the right place is secondary to giving patients the proper care.

In one *manufacturing company*, controlling the inventory in the storeroom and on the shop floor may be the critical factor in the company's success, despite the fact that there are many other systems needed—payroll, accounting, order processing and purchasing. These other systems are certainly important, but the flow and control of inventory make the difference between profit and loss.

Another *manufacturing company* down the street may *not* view inventory as a critical system if the cost of materials is not a major factor in the product. For example, a company makes specialty clamps, but the engineering and quotation systems are the mission-critical areas of the company. If they can't design and quote a custom order quickly, all the inventory in the world doesn't matter.

For a *law firm*, time is an essential part of the product, so its time and billing system is the heart of the organization. This system couldn't operate without an effective means for tracking the human resources of the organization. The firm works with a lot of small clients, so proper accounting of the firm's resources (the people) is vital.

A *telephone company* may have a number of systems, but the billing system is critical to its success. Imagine a company telling its customers they couldn't get call detail on their bills. Consider the impact on cash flow if the bills took six months to produce!

To a *wholesale distribution company*, knowing what is in stock at what price and at which location might be the critical portion of the business, relegating the other systems in comparison. If the product can't be quoted and delivered, the company can't sell.

In some cases, companies within the same industry may have different mission-critical systems. For example, one toy manufacturer may focus on quality control and premium products while the other focuses on producing large quantities inexpensively and efficiently, even if a few of the toys are mediocre.

Each company should define its own priorities and mission-critical systems before purchasing large amounts of technology. The mission-critical systems within your company should be the main target for improvements with computers and information-sharing among those computers. Improve the mission-critical systems, and the entire organization will benefit.

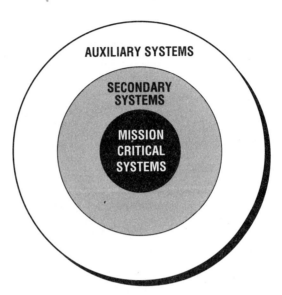

Figure 2.1   Bull's eye! Target your key systems.

Many times a minor improvement in one of the critical areas will outweigh major improvements made in a secondary or nonessential area. For example, in a manufacturing firm whose product cost is 80 percent purchased materials, a 5 percent inventory reduction will far outweigh the advantages of using a word processor to produce letters 50 percent faster. The word-processing benefits might be easier to accomplish, but which one will have the larger impact on the organization's bottom-line profitability?

Example 1: Noncritical Automation: The administrative department of Company A generates 50 letters a week at a cost of $12.50 each (a half hour of time at $25/hour, including wages, benefits and equipment) for a total of $625. An automation project results in cutting the cost in half for a savings of $312.50 per week and a 50 percent decrease in time spent.

Example 2: Mission-Critical Automation: Company B invests in a system to reduce its $5 million inventory by a mere 5 percent, with an inventory carrying cost of 20 percent (interest, storage, obsolescence, etc.). Here, cost savings for a smaller percentage of improvement are much larger—almost $1,000 per week! Side benefits may include less obsolete inventory through more effective ordering methods, and fewer production slowdowns due to shortages. This is the type of bull's eye to shoot for!

If this seems simple, it is. The problem is that most businesses cheerfully ignore such principles in choosing a computer system and in allocating funds for various computer projects. They automate to save clerical costs, and miss the projects that can revolutionize the company!

It takes a committed management team to focus on the critical systems and the improvements that will enhance them. The rewards are high if the systems are executed properly. The risk can be high as well: automating a critical system incorrectly can spell disaster. The implementors of the project must be aware of the impact on the company if things don't work.

If you're just starting out with automation projects, you might consider another approach—a pilot program. This means experimenting by automating a less critical function. This approach carries less risk and may help an organization gain confidence before tackling the major improvements.

The very existence of certain companies depends on their technology, and they have focused their efforts squarely on the mission-critical systems. For example, at Federal Express, knowing the whereabouts of one package (and millions of others at the same time) is *the* mission-critical function. Consequently, packages are controlled by computers at all points of the pickup, routing and delivery process. I once called about an important package and was assured by a person halfway across the country that my package was in the Federal Express truck that was just down the street and would arrive momentarily. It arrived on time as promised. That kind of attention to detail wouldn't have been possible without large investments in technology.

Another example: I use a California bank. On a recent trip to Seattle, I ran short of cash. I noticed one of my bank's automatic tellers near the hotel where I was staying, and the situation was immediately remedied. This simple and convenient transaction would be impossible without a large integrated network of computers that spans the entire West Coast. The bank further capitalizes on this essential network by advertising these services.

Your mission-critical application needn't be a magnificent project that costs millions of dollars and takes years to build. An effective solution can be a simple one. For example, one small software company I talk with frequently on the phone keeps its customers' telephone numbers on line with the receptionists in a simple computerized Rolodex program. This saves its busy customers the extra time necessary to repeat their telephone numbers dozens of times a year. The fact that this company takes the responsibility for knowing them engenders a feeling of quality, efficiency and involvement with its customers.

Finding That Critical System

If you think about it for a moment, your mission-critical areas will surface. What is the most important activity in the organization? What tips the scale in terms of profits and losses? Where do the most painful events occur, and which areas of the business get the closest scrutiny? The answers to these questions will lead you to the areas of the company that deserve the first analysis for improvement. If the mission-critical systems are running perfectly and need no attention, congratulations! You can take your time and introduce technology to help the other systems within your organization at your own pace.

Where Can a Network Save Me Money?

Now that you've learned where to focus your technical improvements, let's take a look at the benefits that can be obtained by using a network in those areas. In one company I worked with, keeping personnel head count down through the use of technology was critical, since running out of office space would force the company to move during a period of high growth. At another company I worked with, business was cyclical, so keeping fixed expenses low was very important. Look carefully at the benefits in terms of your organization's needs and priorities.

Time Is Money

In most organizations, *people* represent a large share of controllable costs. Having productive workers goes a long way toward solving other problems. Sharing information among individuals can save large blocks of their time if properly implemented.

Sharing Information: One company I worked with had two computers dedicated to accounting and invoicing; they weren't connected. This forced the accountant to enter cash received into two separate systems (redundant work); she had to wait for the person at the other computer to go to lunch or go home so she could use that system. It was actually more convenient when the other person was sick! A properly implemented network would allow a single posting of cash, as well as continuous access to the same information by both individuals.

Waiting in Line: In many of the companies I've visited, there is one piece of equipment that everyone needs to use at the same time— for example, a laser printer or color plotter. I've heard some great jokes, good fishing stories, the sports results from the previous day and other information while waiting to use these overworked devices. A network can be set up to share these devices easily and without interruption to others.

Timely Executive Information: How much time does someone in your organization spend trying to tie together the numbers for the company? With a network and the right business software, information about the company can be at the fingertips of the people who make decisions. For example, SBT offers an accounting software series with a business summary screen that shows orders taken, product shipped, purchase orders placed, cash collected and an abundance of other information about the company. If the person running the organization is hooked into the network, it's easy to keep abreast of what is happening.

Schedule Differences: Ever work on the night shift and have to exchange information, like trains in the night, with someone while you're walking out and they're walking in? And what happens when a pivotal person is out of town? Electronic mail can help resolve these problems. For example, messages can be sent as events and problems occur, providing the next shift with a better idea of what happened. A traveling executive can remain in touch by using a portable computer and modem from a hotel room. On a recent two-day trip to North Carolina, I was involved via E-mail in several key company decisions; I was able to contribute without being there.

Documentation: Have you ever gotten results radically different from what you expected when you gave someone verbal instructions on a complex task? Electronic records, such as fax copy, provide documentation that's especially helpful for projects spanning an extended period and involving many people and complex details.

Meeting Avoidance: I can't count the number of unnecessary meetings that I've attended, especially in companies that didn't have an electronic mail facility. With electronic mail, many simple decisions can be reached and information disseminated without having a meeting, saving hundreds of hours of people time per month.

Phone Costs: How many times a day do your customers call up with a question? How many times do you take down the information requested, find an answer and call them back? How much time and money would you save if you had the information necessary to handle the problem immediately? How much goodwill would you spread to your customers?

Reducing Paper Work: Computer companies have been promoting the paperless office for years, but it hasn't materialized yet. Proper networking can reduce the amount of paper work generated, especially for the areas of the company that aren't suited for paper work— the shipping and receiving docks, factory floor and other areas. I installed a high-volume order processing system, using a PC network, that eliminated three days from the order cycle because information was passed electronically between departments rather than by the traditional paper order-and-approval process.

Transfer Costs: If your organization, like many others, uses standalone PCs, you probably spend a good deal of time copying information to floppy disks to give to other people. A network can allow fast transfer of information among machines within a network, saving considerable time. If you're connected to other networks within your organization, located across the country, you can save significantly on the costs of overnight delivery of information and on phone calls between sites. Low-priority transfers can be done at night when phone rates are much lower.

Standardizing: Do you have several computers in use within your company? Are they all different, requiring weeks or months to understand all the subtle differences? A properly implemented network eliminates the hodgepodge of mixed systems and software. All the computers work the same. This can save a lot of time and energy within the organization.

Equipment Savings

You might assume that purchasing a network solution means adding equipment to what you already have, right? Not always. In many cases, a network can justify itself solely on *equipment savings*. Let's look at some examples.

Hardware

If you have several computers and no network, you probably have several different printers—possibly very expensive ones.

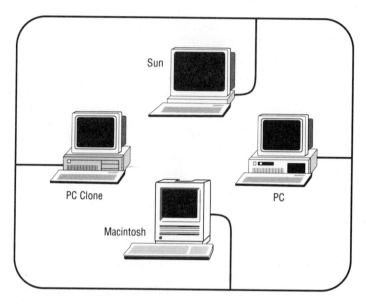

Figure 2.2   A hybrid solution: mixing and matching.

For example, a law firm purchased 16 computers along with 16 HP LaserJet printers for a word processing pool; the operators sat side by side in a large bullpen-type office. The printers cost about $2,000 each, and the effective utilization of each was only about 10 percent. The company could have installed a network (even a simple printer-sharing network), saved thousands of dollars and received greater capabilities.

Another company I worked with saved over $1,000 per person for a five- to six-person group of telephone receptionists using a network file server and "diskless" workstations. (A diskless workstation is a fully powered PC without a floppy or hard-disk drive, drawing its operating programs, applications software and information from the hard drive on the server. More on this in Chapter 8.) In addition to being less expensive, the workstations were simpler to operate than fully configured personal computers, so training costs for this group were cut significantly. All the workstations drew upon a common database, so maintenance was reduced as well.

Software

Using network versions of software can cut cost per user and avoid installation time. For example, a leading dBASE III Plus compatible product is FoxBASE, available in both single-user and multi-user versions. The single-user version costs $395 and must be installed on each personal computer. The multi-user version costs $595 for an unlimited server version. With a 20-person network, this could result in a large savings ($7,000-plus), as well as giving everyone on the network access to the same databases.

Utilization

Sharing expensive devices through networking can result in getting better utilization out of fewer devices. If you have 20 stand-alone personal computers, each one will need access to a printer. To cover these needs, some organizations purchase a number of inexpensive dot matrix printers, which are slow and produce marginal output, and therefore aren't used much. With a network (either a print-sharing network or a complete network), the organization could instead purchase one or two laser printers, saving money overall, and getting better and faster output at the same time.

Mixing the Old with the New

Phasing in new equipment can extend the life of old equipment. The company I work for has a very large network (350-plus personal computers). Since installing the network, we haven't had to discard a single IBM-compatible computer; even the very slow PC-compatible workstations from 1984 can work effectively as low-volume network stations. New equipment is given to the people who need the enhanced speed of 286 and 386 machines, but the people using the older equipment still have access to network resources such as large disks, laser printers, database applications and electronic mail.

Data Integrity and Control

Avoiding Inaccurate Data: How often do you have to get up and go over to another machine to do something you can't do on yours? With a network, common data can be maintained in one central place. This can save on disk space and ensure that everyone is working with accurate, up-to-the-minute copies of the same data. Many organizations will maintain a data file on one machine, and pass around updates once a week. During the week, inaccuracies inevitably develop, causing minor or major problems.

Better Control: By establishing one control point with automated cross-checks, much stricter control over vital data can be accomplished with a network than with stand-alone personal computers. The data are in one central spot where they can be shared, audited and backed up.

Simultaneous Access: Ever have to wait to get to information that you need immediately? A full network allows concurrent access to data by many people for many different uses: one person may be running an aging receivables report, while another is looking up an individual balance, while the president is doing an overall cash report—each from a separate PC on the network but using the same up-to-the-minute information.

Backups/Security

Re-creating Data: Have you had to re-create any data lately? The cost is very high. One company lost an entire month's invoices and had to re-create them from reports and scraps of paper lying around the office. Re-creating data is very expensive, as well as being possibly inaccurate and certainly time-consuming.

In my experience, backups on PCs aren't done very well in most companies, regardless of whether they're used for casual word processing or critical financial analysis.

Networks provide the capability for an effective backup strategy, as long as you have the discipline and the vision to use it.

Security: Look around your organization and imagine what would happen if a disgruntled employee who had just been fired decided to delete some vital information. A network server can be secured, if necessary, and can facilitate redundant backups and provide better security than stand-alone computers. How much is this worth to your organization?

Responsibility: In most organizations, everyone is responsible for doing their own backups, and this typically results in unsatisfactory, incomplete or nonexistent backups. With a network, this task is usually assigned to one individual, or can be made the responsibility of both the user and the network administrator.

Productivity

Providing an effective way to share information can increase productivity. This is an important benefit—now and in the future.

Distributed Environment: A network allows your organization to be distributed in a number of ways. Even when an executive is traveling, he or she can be only a phone call away with a lap-top computer and modem. Business decisions and transactions that would normally have to wait can be made via electronic mail. Organizations with multiple office locations can exchange messages in E-mail in groups, saving phone costs and enhancing communications.

Handling Growth: Once the proper means for sharing information is established, additional people can be added. The largest network I've installed grew from 35 PCs when I arrived to over 400 PCs (and is still growing). New personnel can immediately communicate with everyone in the company (in multiple locations, both national and international).

The Future: The final chapter of this book deals with the future of networking and where technology is going over the next several years. Soon, being connected in the office will also mean being connected to the business world. Electronic Document Interchange (EDI) promises to further reduce paper work between companies: purchase orders and a host of other documents will be sent and received electronically. Although many companies will continue the traditional ways of doing things, the big productivity gains will come from automated businesses.

That's All Great, but What Does My Organization Need?

The chart at the end of this section gives a simplified analysis of the options available to most organizations. These options, along with their associated pluses and minuses, are explored in more detail in Chapter 4. From the chart, you can sort out some options for your organization that provide a skeleton for further investigation. If your needs are at the top of the chart, the solution will be near the top of the technical progression chart. If your needs are extremely complex, move toward the bottom of the technical progression chart.

If you're in the middle, you'll quickly see that you have many options open to you. Most will work well, but there's usually one that's the best fit for a particular organization's current and future needs. If you can find that solution, the fit will be that much better.

Once you've investigated the option that looks most sensible for your organization, you can develop a plan for buying and implementing a system that suits your business.

In making your decision, the better you can identify your business requirements, the better you can match the technology to your goals. Keep your mission-critical systems in mind at all times; these are the key concepts that allow management to determine the right path to follow.

The array of networking options is dazzling, confusing, and includes overlapping functions in many cases. Carry out the organization planning described in Chapter 3, with special emphasis on your organization's future information and system requirements.

Keep in mind our transportation example from Chapter 1: the top end of the technical capabilities chart could be a bicycle and the bottom entry a Boeing 747!

The listing that follows shows a simple-to-complex progression of business organizations matched with one or two solutions that would be appropriate for its size and requirements.

Description	Solution
Little Billy's lemonade stand	No automation needed
Small CPA firm: spreadsheets; word processing; single-user database	Stand-alone PCs
Small publishing company: 10 PCs; shared printers	PCs with print-sharing device
	PCs with zero-slot or serial LAN
Small law firm: 20 PCs; shared printers; file transfer	Single-file-server full LAN

Small software company: 20 computer users; shared printers; file transfer; E-mail; applications	Small minicomputer, multi-user PC or multiple-file-server LAN
Factory or small college: 200 computer users; shared printers; file transfer; E-mail; distributed applications	LAN with medium to large minicomputer integrated
Airline reservations system: 1,000 computer users, performing the same tasks	Large-scale minicomputers or mainframe processing capability

---

Phasing in Your Plan (Bet a Little, Win a Little, Bet a Little More...)

Many companies dive into an automation plan with total abandon, like someone who's just found a hobby or a new love. There's great excitement and anticipation; large amounts of money are spent. But a few months later (sometimes weeks), the fun is over, the money is gone, the results are disappointing, the benefits are largely unrealized, and everyone is wondering what went wrong.

One way to avoid this scenario is to phase in your solution in stages. You still have a business to run. You don't want to disrupt normal activities. Cash flow is probably one of your biggest headaches. The last thing your company or department needs is a $19,000 outlay. By taking things one step at a time, you can reconcile all of the above.

In some cases, this just isn't possible. If your company is growing exponentially, you might not be able to wait for a phased solution. If you purchase a large minicomputer and software package, you have a single major project on your hands. But for most organizations, phasing in a solution is the best way to minimize the risk and avoid some pain.

A pilot project (described earlier) should be used to test the soundness of the plan you've developed. A portion of the overall project should be selected and implemented. Items such as response time, ease of use and real versus projected costs will surface during this pilot project. Allow adjustments in expectations for the remaining phases of the plan.

At this point in the game, you can stop and ask yourself the following questions: Did it take more or less time to implement than you anticipated? Have you achieved more or less in benefits than you expected? Did it cost more or less than you planned for?

If you're happy with the initial results, you can easily go on to additional phases. If you're not satisfied, you have lost some time and money, but in comparison to your losses if an entire project had bombed, you've suffered only a minor setback.

Subsequent phases can be more encompassing and take more time. Each phase can build on the prior phase, while leaving open the options of discontinuing or retreating without losing existing benefits. If the phases are completed in the order of greatest benefit to the organization, later phases can be delayed, eliminated or accelerated, based on how well the first phases are working.

Learning from the Successes

If your organization has successfully used technology in the past, take a few moments to analyze why. What items made people perceive that a success had been realized? More output? The same answers in a shorter period of time? The capability for multiple iterations quickly? A reduction in the number of people necessary to do a particular task? The ability to accomplish things that were impossible previously?

Apply this knowledge to projections for improvements. Look for areas where technology will be likely to succeed later on—in view of the way technology has changed the business already and how the organization perceives the technological innovations.

Learning from the Failures

Everyone likes success stories, and you're likely to hear them repeated time after time (sometimes they're like fish stories, growing in magnitude as time goes on). Not as comforting but even more valuable are the attempts at automation that failed. Whether it was an out-and-out failure (it didn't work, and it wouldn't work anywhere) or a localized failure (it didn't work here, regardless of the success that was obtained elsewhere), it's still important for analysis.

Sometimes it's hard to gather information about the failures: the decision-makers have moved on to other companies or don't seem to remember the complete circumstances connected with the situation. If you can dig deep enough, however, you'll get some valuable information on what to avoid in the future.

Try to understand whether the failure was technical (the equipment couldn't support the desired results), organizational (the people wouldn't support the automation effort) or simply a misdirected project (it wasn't important enough to command the attention of the people who could make it work).

Moving On

In this chapter, we've looked at two important elements to consider in your decision-making process: mission-critical systems and potential benefits from a solution that enables shared information. After a thorough examination of these areas, if you feel that your organization is doing pretty well, you might want to stop right here and spend the same money for other business improvements. (When was the last time anyone told you that?)

At the risk of sounding repetitious, do what is best for your organization from a business standpoint (you'll be chanting this maxim by the end of the book). Don't get caught up in the technology or the vendor hoopla. Take a detached view of the technology and relate the benefits to your own organization. Take a dash of someone else's success, mix it with a proven solution, blend in one dedicated vendor, and add a generous portion of objective pessimism. Shape the ingredients into a compress and apply only to the parts of the organization that can benefit (usually not the ones where the complaining is the loudest!).

If you're convinced that you need to share information within your company, read on. The next chapter will help you formulate a plan of attack, focusing mostly on current capabilities and future needs.

Developing a plan is a vital step, and not one to be taken lightly or delegated down to the bottom echelon. If the plan matches the true current and future needs of the business, many of the pitfalls will be eliminated, and the odds will be stacked in your favor.

3

Building the Information Plan

Building an information plan is the first thing a company must do to determine its networking needs. Even though you may not have the expertise of an MIS director, who can determine exactly which hardware and software configurations are best, your information plan will set the stage for implementation and help ensure success.

In this chapter, you'll focus on long-range planning. Although you might want to skip this and move directly into more "hands-on" information, I'm personally asking you to read it several times and do the planning outlined. It will be worth the time spent if you can avoid one small mistake when you implement your network.

I've witnessed many project failures (and participated in a few!) where people installed computers, networks and other pieces of technology without adequate planning.

Poor planning can cause your system to fail for a number of reasons:

1. The initiator/implementor didn't explain to management all the issues and costs associated with a project, thus setting a level of expectation that could not be met within the allocated budget.

2. It's discovered after the fact that computer A can't be connected to software B, or that an entire part-numbering system must be revamped in order to automate because the new system allows only 12 digits.

3. The unique needs of the business weren't taken into account when deciding on what was to be accomplished, resulting in a solution for a nonexistent or secondary problem.

One manufacturing company that I know of purchased a complete manufacturing and financial system without taking the time to make a thorough evaluation of its needs and the available options.

Deep into the implementation, the staff discovered that the new system failed to accomplish what was needed most—tracking its products from receipt of material, through the manufacturing process to the finished goods. The result was wasted implementation time and the additional expense of modifying the new package.

4. No one established priorities or guidelines for measuring whether a project was a success or failure and when to stop.

For example, a small company purchased a ten-user network for its routine business transactions and experienced a great return. The administrator—thinking that if a little was good, more would be better—talked management into purchasing a number of expensive add-ons to the network. The result was overkill. The network ultimately cost much more than it was worth because the solutions outnumbered the problems. Stop when you're ahead!

Holding Back and Making a Plan

It always seems easier to take some immediate steps toward solving problems. Well-thought-out decisions can help you avoid investing a lot of time and money in equipment that will have to be discarded within a year.

One of the best ways to ensure success with projects involving automation is to make each piece of the project build on the other. This requires a carefully orchestrated plan.

Before making a large number of hardware or software acquisitions, you should take a long look at what you're trying to accomplish and identify the vital components of success. Based on this, an information plan can be developed that will focus resources on the most important items.

If you're inclined to doubt that a carefully written, comprehensive analysis is what your company needs, in view of its pressing information demands, consider the process of building or expanding your house when you find out you're going to have a child. You might be desperate for a new bedroom for the upcoming arrival, but you probably wouldn't try to solve the problem by going to the local hardware store and purchasing a pile of miscellaneous wood, nails, paint and carpet. Think about the logical way to approach that project: you'd seek out an architect, draw up some plans, consult with contractors, get quotes, sign a contract, schedule the work, etc.

A similar approach is needed for your computer and information systems.

What do you do first to build an information plan? Exactly what you would do if you were renovating your house. Let's develop an outline of the plan, listing only the major subheadings required at this point, then concentrate on each category, one at a time, explaining the vital points and how they apply to several different types of companies. (For a related questionnaire, please see page 51.)

BUSINESS SUMMARY/GOALS

▲ Current Information Systems Summary

▲ Mission-Critical Systems Analysis

▲ Realistic Budget Assessment and Justification

▲ Information Systems Goals

▲ Risk Factors/Contingency Plans

▲ Impact of Future Growth

Caveat: Your organization may use a different type of planning process. The format is not vitally important; the key is to take the time and do the thinking and planning necessary to ensure success. The essentials could easily be outlined on the back of a napkin; I've seen elaborate, beautifully presented plans that said very little and missed the critical elements.

Business Summary/Goals

If your organization is good at planning, there will already be an overall business plan to draw from for this information. I am amazed, however, at the number of companies that don't seem to have any overall strategic plan for their management or employees to refer to. The business summary describes the business in terms of its products, services, annual sales, major markets, market volatility and many other items.

Without a plan or blueprint for the future, picking technology is almost a shot in the dark. You can easily overestimate growth and purchase a solution that saps your organization's profits. Conversely, underestimating growth can cause the chosen solution to be inadequate at the most critical moment. All things considered, however, too little is better than too much. If your company's growth exceeds expectations, at least you'll have extra funds for playing catch-up.

Mission-critical systems should be referenced in every section of the plan. If they're properly identified and planned, little else can prevent an organization from meeting its goals. Let's look at the business summary for an accounting consulting firm.

Overview

ABC Accounting is a firm that specializes in complex tax accounting and financial planning for clients with incomes over $500K per year. Its critical mission is providing clients with the most up-to-date and accurate advice possible. A current business summary with projections for the coming year is as follows:

ITEM	1989 TOTALS	1990 GOALS
Sales	1.6 million	2.4 million
Personnel	8	10
Profits	170,000	260,000
Customers	275	450

Strategic Planning Elements for 1990

Personnel: A significant gain in personnel productivity is expected during the year as a result of the installation of computer systems.

Increasing productivity within the space constraints of the current office is a critical issue. Failure to reach this goal will result in a disruptive and expensive move.

Also, several key employees will be retiring. Documenting their knowledge and cross-training people who'll be replacing them are vital to the company's ongoing success.

Customers: ABC Accounting is planning to increase its customer base dramatically in 1990. Since this will be done after the tax season, revenue for the new customers will be low, but it should rise rapidly during the following year. An aggressive marketing campaign will start in June.

Outside Access: Several of the key information sources that the company uses are now available via a personal computer and modem, allowing the company to gather information at a much faster rate and at lower costs.

Current Information Systems Summary

The current information systems summary is exactly what it sounds like—a synopsis of the company's existing methods/systems for processing and organizing its information. The current method may be manual, automated or a mixture of both.

Many businesses use outside service bureaus for processing such items as payroll and complex inventory planning. A realistic assessment should be given of how well each system is working and is expected to work when viewed in a future perspective. All systems should be realistically evaluated; in some cases existing systems may be costing more than they're worth.

Getting a good idea of your current costs is also important to this type of summary. It's easy to underestimate the amount being spent on various functions that could be automated or done in a more cost-effective way. How much does it cost to process an order manually? What is the real cost of maintaining up-to-date manual engineering drawings? What are the hidden costs? How many are being processed per month or week, and how is that number going to change?

In many organizations, the best way to research existing information systems is to look at forms currently in use, clipboards and notebook logs hanging around the company and, of course, the already computerized functions. Using a checklist like the following one can help; it contains basic functions common to most organizations. Some information systems might need to be broken down into subsystems if your organization is particularly complex in one area or another. (For a related in-depth questionnaire, please see page 51.)

SYSTEM	PRESENT METHOD	APPROXIMATE COST	PRIORITY	LEVEL OF SATISFACTION
Order Entry				
Invoicing				
Inventory Control				
Bill of Materials				
Job Costing				
Purchasing				
Time & Billing				
Document Management				
General Ledger				
Accounts Payable				
Accounts Receivable				
Fixed Assets				
Payroll				
Human Resource Management				

Hardware and Software Summary

Take an inventory of all the hardware and software presently in use in your organization. This will give you a good idea of usage, trends and preferences that already exist. (For an in-depth checklist, please see pages 54–57.)

HARDWARE	SOFTWARE
✔ Description	✔ Name
✔ Age	✔ Version
✔ Value	✔ Value
✔ Importance	✔ Importance
✔ Usage	✔ Usage
✔ Upgrade possibilities	✔ Number of people using

Let's look at a hypothetical case: the current information systems summary for a fictitious manufacturing company that contracts with the government to produce munitions.

Overview

"Bill's Bombs" started as a small company, but has grown very rapidly. Bill had previously been a distributor of fireworks. He decided to take some chemistry classes and came up with an advanced formula for artillery shells that he was able to sell to the government on a long-term contract. His business has grown rapidly, to around $20 million per year, with employee head count spiraling upwards as well. A summary of the current information systems follows:

Order Entry: A simple handwritten ledger is used, since only a few orders are received per year. The cost is very low and this method seems completely satisfactory.

Invoicing: It's currently done by hand and requires two accounting clerks and 25 percent of the controller's time (at $80K per year). Invoices are closely tied to the production process; they must reference the batch number and lot number of the munitions.

Inventory Control: This function is currently handled on a single Apple II within the production area at an approximate cost of $45K per year. It's given high priority. The frustration level is equally high, since other people in the company cannot access the information at the same time and must rely on outdated reports produced every couple of days. Since the Apple is not compatible with the other personal computers within the company, information must be printed on paper and re-entered, often resulting in errors and taking a lot of time.

Bills of Materials: These are very simple bills, done by hand at a cost of under $10K per year. Occasionally, discrepancies between the handwritten bills and the bills in the inventory computer cause inventory shortages.

Job Costing: Costing is done, prior to invoicing, on an additional PC in accounting. This takes up a tremendous amount of time and demands complete accuracy because of government auditing. Discrepancies often arise: inventory systems don't match the physical inventory, or the manual purchasing records don't match the records in the inventory system.

Purchasing: Purchasing is done by hand, using the bill of materials and the purchase list produced by the inventory computer. The cost is low, due to a minimal number of parts, but the satisfaction level is low as well, due to shortages and the constant need to expedite deliveries from vendors.

Time and Billing: Does not apply for this company.

General Ledger: The controller does this using Lotus. While this method works well, there are no controls on his spreadsheets; consequently, mistakes in balancing the business are difficult to track.

Accounts Payable: Payables are done by hand at a minimal cost ($15K). This area works adequately due to the small number of purchases made.

Accounts Receivable: The controller personally takes care of accounts receivable. This system works very well in its manual mode since the only customer is the government. Occasional prodding to process invoices submitted for payment is necessary, but there is no problem with eventually getting paid except in the case of invoices incorrectly submitted by the invoicing clerks.

Fixed Assets: These are also handled by the controller, using Lotus. This is a reasonably priced system; and due to the low volume of new purchases, it works well for the company.

Payroll: This is done at a service bureau for a very minimal cost.

Human Resource Management: The work is done by hand and involves minimal cost.

Based on the information presented, it's easy to see that most of the expenditures should be aimed at tying together the inventory, job costing and invoicing functions. This will save time, give greater customer satisfaction, and allow management information to be generated quickly and accurately.

Mission-Critical Systems Analysis

As you learned in Chapter 2, identifying your mission-critical systems is a vital step that requires enough soul-searching to be able to define those areas that are most essential to your company's success.

Isolating these factors and focusing on enhancing their performance or lowering their cost is the best way to ensure the success of a project. Too often the focus is on solving problems that aren't vital to the organization's success, or trying to solve all problems equally, resulting in an equal amount of resources applied to critical and noncritical applications alike.

Having trouble getting a handle on your mission-critical systems? Get the key people from the organization in a room for an hour or so and identify these systems through a process of elimination. Look at all existing systems and find reasons why each one is or is not critical to the company's survival. The mission-critical systems will emerge as the ones you really can't do without.

Try the lifeboat drill at your next management meeting. Take all the systems you have, put them in a theoretical lifeboat, and start tossing the noncritical ones overboard. When you get down to the last two or three, you will have your mission-critical systems identified.

Let's take a nonprofit organization as an example and locate the mission-critical systems. Jim Smith is the director of a local foundation dedicated to preserving historical monuments within a 100-mile area. The foundation is supported solely by gifts from donors from all over the country. It's easy to identify the mission-critical imperatives here: stay in touch with the donors and maintain a database of current and future historical sites. The accounting functions can probably be done in a simple checkbook format; inventory might be limited to some paint, stamps and office supplies.

In the preceding example, the mission-critical systems emerged immediately from a one- or two-sentence description of the organization. This will usually be the case; in most organizations, a concise description will point to the mission-critical systems.

Realistic Budget Assessment and Justification

This is the area where many organizations get hung up in their planning, mostly because it's difficult to grapple with. Obviously, everyone wants to spend the smallest amount possible and garner the most benefits, but setting a reasonable level of expenditures for information systems projects seems to be a difficult assignment.

Estimating the benefits is still more difficult, since they're usually "softer" in nature than the costs. Establishing a reasonable level of expenditures and expectations can keep a project on track and allow all involved participants to measure progress.

In many companies, projects are done in a reactionary manner, aimed at solving a problem that has recently arisen and is causing strife or pain within the organization. The benefit desired is a return to some semblance of order in that area of the organization.

Other businesses focus on proactive systems, solving problems before they reach the "meltdown" stage. It's especially important for planners to identify technology that can grow with the future needs of the organization.

For example, a book publishing company recently networked three computers together during a period of slow growth, because they anticipated the business spurt that would ensue when six additional titles were published. You don't want to go fiddling around with new systems and technology when all your employees are maxed out trying to meet heavy demand.

Budgets or scheduled expenditures can take several forms:

For a *specific project*, a complete definition of costs and benefits can be estimated and tracked: $10,000 for the hardware, $4,000 for the software, $6,000 for training, conversion and implementation costs, and $200 a month for maintenance and supplies. These estimates might define the entire scope of an information systems project designed to bring bill-of-materials processing in-house rather than using an outside service bureau.

The benefits might include elimination of service bureau processing costs ($3,000 per month—a tangible benefit), and the advantage of having current, up-to-the minute information (a softer, less tangible benefit). Many companies calculate savings only on the visible or "hard" benefits, simply absorbing the "soft" or intangible benefits within the organization. In many cases, the soft benefits, if thoroughly analyzed, far outweigh the tangible benefits. In most cases, successful systems allow the organization to move to the next level of sophistication rather than simply cutting costs.

If the implementation above took three months, and all of the costs/benefits were realized, the project would pay for itself in a seven- to eight-month period after implementation. (Savings of $3,000 minus $200 for supplies gives a net savings of $2,800 per month after the third month.)

For a *broader project* and ongoing systems efforts, another method used for budgeting is based on a percentage of total sales. Industry averages are available indicating the amount of revenue spent on total information processing within a business, typically 1 percent on the low side (e.g., restaurants, dry cleaners) to a large percentage on the high side (insurance companies spend a large portion of revenue on information processing).

Another method used by many companies is the *fixed resource* approach: a certain amount of money is set aside for automation within the organization, and some human resources are identified as well. The individuals responsible for making the systems work do the best they can with what they have, adding additional resources as results are obtained.

Many business schools would call this poor management, since it lacks the rigorous pay-back analysis and doesn't constitute much forward planning. In fact, this is the predominant method of allocating resources that I've encountered in smaller organizations. If these limited resources are focused on the mission-critical areas of the business and guided by senior management, the contribution level can be tremendous in relation to the amount invested.

Information Systems Goals

Defining appropriate goals for an information system is one of the most positive items that can be accomplished by a management team. With definite goals, the individuals involved with making the solutions work will have a clear target to shoot for, rather than the nonspecific goal of "making things better" or "raising productivity." Goals such as cutting three days out of a 14-day order cycle, or cutting material costs by 25 percent can be clearly understood, worked toward and later measured to determine results obtained.

Whenever possible, goals should be specific and targeted, with small subgoals outlined as well.

Overall Goal

A 5 percent increase in overall profitability for an automobile parts store. Sales are stable, so cost decreases must be sought through automation within the store.

Subgoals

1. Reduce inventory of parts that aren't selling quickly: a six-month supply may amount to only two parts if only one of these parts is sold every three months.

2. Identify historically busy times of the day so that counter salespeople can be scheduled accordingly.

3. Obtain larger purchasing discounts by ordering larger quantities of the parts that sell quickly.

4. Bar-code all inventory to avoid customer ill will and costly returns when a similar part is substituted by mistake. Expedite the process of taking inventory, eliminating the need to shut down twice a year for one day.

You won't get a lot of direction from the overall goal, but the subgoals should trigger vivid pictures of computer systems that will help you to meet the overall goal.

An additional benefit of identifying specific subgoals is that they'll help you and your vendor evaluate your needs and various solutions. If the vendor proposes a system that doesn't fulfill those needs, the proposal can be easily eliminated, no matter what dazzling array of hardware or exotic software is presented.

As an example, one of your subgoals might be better control of your inventory of special gears used in engines. These items have individual serial numbers so that they can be tracked by engine and car. If serialized inventory is critical, this requirement can be transferred to a standardized plan given to vendors, and used to quickly screen proposed solutions.

Risk Factors/Contingency Plans

In this section, the preparer should examine the amount of risk involved with the organization's information systems. If they were suddenly incapacitated, would the organization still be able to function? Different companies have different requirements: a retail store might have the luxury of closing down if the lights went off, while the same options don't exist for a hospital or police department.

I have witnessed companies that were paralyzed due to a hard-disk failure, with no backups of critical information such as pending orders or payments. One company had come to rely on an inexpensive PC clone for all shipment and order information, and had neglected to back up the computer since installing the system. When the hard-disk unit failed, little information was available on paper with which to reconstruct months of history.

Another company did all the right backups and stored them next to the personal computer that held all the information about the company. If the computer had broken down, they would have been in great shape; however, that wasn't the problem they encountered. Their office was burglarized, and the fireproof box of backup disks was taken along with the computer.

A good risk analysis/contingency plan would have noted the importance of backups, as well as recommending that the PC be a high-quality one (with another machine nearby that could be called into service if necessary). Keeping copies of backups off-site is also very important in ensuring that your information survives.

The amount of time you spend on contingency planning should be in direct proportion to how much risk your organization can absorb without major disruption. For many companies, planning an adequate backup program is sufficient. For companies that need systems that work despite almost all obstacles, this planning must become much more detailed and comprehensive. A number of items that can be accomplished toward this end are discussed in later chapters.

Impact of Future Growth

The future growth section of the information plan details exactly what it implies: the forecast of how much growth the company expects to encounter and how this growth will impact the organization's information systems.

This can be a critical area for many companies, affecting the overall strategy tremendously. If growth of 75 percent is anticipated, selecting a solution that will handle only current business would be expensive and disruptive; the company would outgrow the solution before it could be implemented. If growth means distributing the organization to multiple locations (remote sales offices, regional warehouses or factories), the systems chosen must be able to work in all the environments.

If the business is stable, the plan for the organization should probably be stable as well, minimizing large outlays, if possible, and implementing the system smoothly and without disruption. Another factor to consider is complexity of information: in some cases, the amount of information required by a company will rise exponentially when business increases by a relatively small percentage or when the organization goes into a different type of product.

Let's use a finished-goods manufacturer as an example. Previously, the company purchased several large subassemblies from various suppliers, tied them together by means of some special software, and sold the product for a healthy profit margin. In an attempt to make even more profits, management now plans to build the major subassembly at the factory that used to do only final assembly and distribution. Final sales remain stable, but the amount of information processing goes up dramatically. Additional inventory items must be ordered, inspected and warehoused, complex shop-floor tracking is required, and multilevel bills of materials are needed, in addition to tracking the maintenance requirements of a large number of fabrication machines. In a case like this, management could grossly underestimate the change needed for vital information systems, thereby causing the new strategy to fail.

Obviously, future growth potential should play an important role in your planning analysis. You don't need a crystal ball to figure out many of the factors that need to be considered in relation to future growth.

Tying It All Together

To help you with each step toward building an information plan, refer to the following questions and checklists.

Business Summary and Goals

- What is your primary product or service?
- Who are your primary customers?
- What are your sales figures for the past three years?
- How many employees do you have?
- Is the company growing, shrinking or stable?
- What does management want the company to do?
- What is the business structure—corporation, partnership, sole proprietor?
- How many locations are there?
- What does the future look like?
- Where are profits derived?
- Who are your competitors?
- What is the size of the total market for this product or service?
- How much market share do you have?
- What is your volume for the following common business transactions?
    - orders and order lines, per order • phone calls • faxes
    - inventory parts received, issued • checks received
    - checks written, invoices received/produced • shipments
    - memos • labor hours • accounts payable vouchers
    - customer additions, changes or deletions
    - projects completed • payroll checks
- What are your business hours?
- Is your business local, regional, national or international?
- What paper work are you required to file regularly for your business?

Current Information Systems Summary

- What hardware do you have?
- What software do you use?
- Which equipment/system works best?
- Which equipment/system gives you the most trouble?

- Is the equipment old or up-to-date?
- Do you thoroughly understand the current systems?
- What changes would you like to make in the software?
- Do current systems address your most important areas?
- How much growth could the current systems handle?
- Could new personnel learn the current systems easily?
- Do system failures ever create critical problems?
- Are the current systems documented?

Mission-Critical Systems Analysis

- Which activity makes the difference between success and failure in your organization?
- How does that activity relate to current systems?
- How could the mission-critical areas of the business be improved?
- Who are the people responsible for the mission-critical systems?
- What factors do you rate your competition on?

Realistic Budget Assessment and Justification

- Where are the bottlenecks within your business?
- How much can you afford to spend?
- What kind of return would you like on projects?
- How much people time can be realistically spent?
- How much can you afford to lose?
- Should you tiptoe or dive in financially?

Information Systems Goals

- Can these goals be quantified and subdivided?
- Are you aiming at improvement or putting out fires?
- Who is responsible for the results?
- Do you know someone else achieving the same goals?

- Does everyone involved feel committed to these goals?
- How are your competitors enhancing their systems?

Risk Factors/Contingency Plans

- What is the worst thing that could happen to your systems?
- Are you prepared to deal with it?
- How much can your business grow?
- What if your sales were cut in half?
- What if your building was destroyed?
- What if the person responsible for the computers quit?
- What if the computer's hard disk crashed?

Impact of Future Growth

- How fast could your business grow?
- Will the new systems last five to seven years?
- Can you afford to change systems again?
- What is the true cost of changing?
- What systems will have to be integrated as time goes on?
- What is happening in your industry?
- What future technology is likely to affect your business?
- How will the following areas be affected if sales double?

  - employees • telephone calls • number of orders
  - number of parts • number of offices
  - hours of operation • facilities • warehouse
  - accounting transactions

HARDWARE INVENTORY CHECKLIST

Inventory number _____

Primary user _____

Primary use _____

Overall description _____
_____

MANUFACTURER

Name _____

Address _____

City, state, zip _____

Phone number _____

Contact _____

Date of purchase _____

Purchase cost _____

MAINTENANCE INFORMATION

Serial number _____

Maintenance phone number _____

Date of contract _____

Contact _____

CONFIGURATION INFORMATION

CPU type and speed _____

Math coprocessor info _____

Type of hard disk—capacity/speed _____

Memory configuration and amount _____

Graphics card and settings _____

Monitor type _____

Network card type and settings _____

Printer info _____

Modem info _____

Mouse info _____

Other devices _____

HISTORICAL NOTES ON MAINTENANCE, CHANGES, ETC.

_____

_____

_____

_____

SOFTWARE INVENTORY CHECKLIST

Inventory number _____

MANUFACTURER

Name _____

Address _____

City, state, zip _____

Phone number _____

Contact _____

Date of purchase _____

Purchase cost _____

MAINTENANCE INFORMATION

Serial number _____

Maintenance phone number _____

Date of contract _____

Contact _____

Original version _____

Current version _____

License restrictions _____

```
┌─────────────────────────────────────────────────┐
│  USER INFORMATION                                 │
│                                                   │
│  Used by      _____    │
│                                                   │
│  Primary purpose  _____    │
│                                                   │
│  Critical items produced  _____    │
│                                                   │
│  Experience level  _____    │
│                                                   │
└─────────────────────────────────────────────────┘
```

Moving On

In this chapter, we've examined a structure for your organization to use in creating an information plan that encompasses the goals of the organization, an evaluation of current information processing, goals for future automation projects, and the contingency planning for emergencies.

If you create this plan, using the method outlined (or your own version), you'll have a set of reference points as you move into implementing new projects. If problems are encountered, trade-offs can be made against the goals outlined by management, not in a vacuum. If things go well, you'll be able to check the gains and outlays against the expected benefits and costs in the plan.

In the next chapter, you'll examine your options, ranging from doing nothing to installing a large-scale minicomputer that will handle all your future information systems. The number of basic options is limited, but each can be integrated in many ways; and combining various options can open almost limitless avenues—to success or failure.

Throughout the remainder of the book, keep your overall plan handy, and revise it often to reflect internal and external changes.

4

Looking at the Options

Now that you've identified the systems within your organization that may be enhanced by networking, let's explore some alternative approaches to sharing information that are currently available.

There are many possibilities; we'll focus on several major solutions available to the small and medium-size business or the department within a large corporation. If you're seriously in need of a mainframe solution, you'll probably have a sophisticated staff to handle the acquisition of that multimillion-dollar technology. But because many organizations already have several layers of technology in place, we'll also consider the merits of a mixed or hybrid solution.

The Options

1. Take small steps and wait for a better solution.
2. Install a local area PC network using MS-DOS.
3. Install a local area PC network using OS/2 servers.
4. Install a Unix-based solution.
5. Install a MacIntosh network.
6. Install a hybrid solution (combining several solutions).
7. Buy a traditional minicomputer.

If you don't already have a solution that your organization is satisfied with or committed to, look at all possible solutions. Too many important strategic and technical decisions have been made based on personal preference rather than on facts and an objective view of what the organization needs.

The computer industry changes so rapidly that almost everything must be questioned when making a decision. This strategic decision shouldn't be delegated to a consultant or a low-level employee in the organization unless management wants to assume full responsibility if failure occurs a few years or months later. (There won't be a problem if it works—dozens of people will be standing in line to take the credit!)

The right decision will be reached by examining and weighing both financial and technical considerations. If a decision is based solely on price, you may find you've purchased a solution that is antiquated and inflexible. On the other hand, you may end up with state-of-the-art equipment that greatly exceeds your budget. Make sure the relevant parties get involved ahead of time rather than after the fact.

On a recent business trip, I met with the president of a small manufacturing company. We discussed his frustration with his information processing strategy. It turned out he had hired someone with a programming background to implement a computer system. This technical person had virtually no background in manufacturing, but was given free rein to make the decision for the company. The programmer simply chose a setup he had worked with previously at other companies. The results were obsolete software and an inadequate system. Now the system was failing, the programmer had complete control, and nobody else had a clue as to how to get the information out of the computer.

Delegate the research if you must, but understand that you may have to live with the decisions long after the implementors have vanished.

With these caveats in mind, let's move on and explore the pros and cons of each solution.

Take Small Steps and Play the Waiting Game

There aren't many areas in business where you're almost assured that prices will decline and performance will improve while you're in the process of making your decision. For a number of years the entire computer hardware and software industry has been in a fierce downward price spiral. The shiny new technology that was yesterday's state-of-the-art equipment is fast becoming obsolete.

Such rapid obsolescence makes it more important than ever to make a decision that fits today's *and* tomorrow's needs. The short-term solution of expanding what you already have can give you more time to analyze your problems and become better informed on how to implement. (Chapter 5 is devoted to short-term hardware and software solutions.)

Pros

If you feel no available solution answers your specific needs, there's nothing wrong with waiting, unless the need for relief is so acute that you must take immediate action. Chances are, someone out there is working on that solution right now. New developments in the hardware, software and networking areas are continuing, yielding solutions that are more functional than ever before.

If you're the president or department manager of your company, and have high-quality, aggressive and technically literate people working for you, this may be an unpopular stance. You may be pressured to go ahead now and make a "few" changes or additions as other solutions become available. It may make sense to implement a partial solution while other options develop, but you should be able to justify the cost of changing over to another system in a few months or a few years.

As an example, I worked for a large, distributed manufacturing company in Bellevue, WA, as the director of technical services. I had been hired to straighten out a series of systems that had been purchased the year before. The purchase looked brilliant: it included solid, reliable hardware combined with a manufacturing system package that would meet most of the needs of six to ten manufacturing units owned by the parent company (most of these units were uncomputerized).

The project had run into implementation problems because everyone assumed the computers would install themselves (at least that's what the vendors had promised), and the one-person "team" trying to make it all work was so overloaded that he had barely gotten started!

I walked in and developed a brilliant plan for making this project work. I submitted a whole list of reasonable (I thought) expenditures, which included hiring five people and buying more hardware. When I presented this plan, the president basically told me to do what I could do with what was already available—no new expenditures. "Wait and see if either technology or time solves our problems instead of spending an additional large amount of capital to force the situation," was all I got for my entire presentation. A year later, we added an additional employee and another computer, hardly the solution I had originally anticipated.

Ultimately, we achieved greater results because of several technical enhancements that came about (some software improvements and favorable hardware prices). In addition, the operating units realized that they didn't need to install every piece of the manufacturing software, only the pieces that were critical to their business.

Patience and the ability of senior management to say no to technical pressure saved big money while still obtaining substantial benefits in the long run.

Cons

You shouldn't wait to update technology if procrastinating would only exacerbate current problems. At the point where you're finally forced to act, you would have to make a snap decision, without sufficient time to properly implement a comprehensive solution.

In some cases, it's simply a matter of compromise. For example, a company that must slash inventory costs cannot afford a protracted decision-making process before automating its inventory systems. The cost of excess inventory must be the overriding concern; even a mediocre solution might pay big dividends. Another example is financial service companies, which have had to make fast decisions in the technical arena in order to stay competitive with others in their industry. And with the rapidly increasing pace of innovation in the personal computer software arena, development of new capabilities for traditional areas is accelerating, making an accurate and quick decision process a necessity.

Install a PC LAN Using MS-DOS

Since 1987, installing a PC-based network using MS-DOS has become a serious option for those interested in linking computers. In fact, PC LANs have become one of the most popular and successful options. Major strides have been made by the network vendors to provide solutions that work effectively and can grow with your company. Let's look at the positive and negative factors involved in installing a PC/MS-DOS network.

Pros

Sharing Information: Information can be shared among the various PCs attached to the network via one or more file servers (other PCs available for use by the machines on the network). These may be dedicated file servers (meaning they're used only for network software) or nondedicated file servers (e.g., performing as a word processor and a server at the same time).

Sharing Devices: Through the network software, users can share printers, plotters, modems, disk drives and other expensive equipment attached to the network. This eliminates the problem of people lining up to use a certain machine that has a laser printer attached, or jockeying for individual modems, even though they may be used five percent of the time or less.

Communications: Attaching all the PCs to the LAN allows communication between machines without the users of those PCs having to leave their desks. This might translate into electronic mail (E-mail) or computer file transfers. E-mail between individuals can raise productivity tremendously by saving communication time, especially when there are schedule conflicts or considerable physical distance between work groups. It can also cut down on meetings when an issue can be resolved with a simple response to a simple question.

Lower Cost/Investment Preservation: If you already have the PCs, setting up a LAN is not nearly as expensive as some other alternatives. The pricing issue can be manipulated to fit the opinion of whomever you may be talking to at the time. My opinion is that this is the least expensive option, particularly if you already have PCs in place in your business and you can finance your LAN in stages.

Incremental Investment: Buying a LAN can be done successfully on a piecemeal basis, adding hardware and software as needed and/or when funds become available. It's ironic that the high-growth businesses that are continually plagued with cash-flow problems are the very ones that need to invest in automating and networking! Buying equipment and services gradually can help on the financial side.

Ease of Implementation and Training: The movement into a PC network is fairly straightforward, since much of it looks and acts like what you already have. The applications that run stand-alone on your existing PCs can still run stand-alone on the network. To ease into the LAN slowly, you could start with sharing some printers, then some E-mail and file transfers. Multi-user applications software can wait until you're comfortable with other facets of network operation.

Widespread Support and Availability: These networks constitute the largest base of network nodes currently in use, so the chances are good that several vendors in your area sell and support LANs using MS-DOS. Another alternative is mail order, which is becoming a popular way of purchasing network hardware and software.

If that all sounds pretty good, it is. But let's look at some of the disadvantages:

Cons

Memory Limitations: MS-DOS has an inherent limitation called "RAM cram," which alludes to the fact that DOS can use only 640K of main computer memory. When DOS was originally conceived, this represents a large amount of memory for the fledgling personal computers it ran on. However, the 640K barrier has quickly become the largest limitation within the PC community. With a PC-based network, the problem becomes even worse. The network software requires that "drivers" be loaded on each machine attached to the network. These drivers allow the attached PCs to communicate with network servers and devices. The drivers take up space when installed in the computer's memory, limiting even further the amount left over for such big, memory-intensive programs as Lotus, Ventura Publisher or AutoCAD.

Some vendors have devised special network interfaces that allow popular network software to be loaded into RAM on the network card rather than using precious memory on the PC. The remaining RAM can be used to buffer information coming into and going out of the PC. These cards are usually more expensive, but they do relieve this problem and provide higher overall performance.

Single-Tasking: MS-DOS is a *single-tasking* operating system, which means it performs only one function at a time. Network operating systems (NOS) for the file servers must be able to respond to multiple "client" requests for services (access to information on disk, information to the printer, etc.).

In order to accomplish this, the major network vendors have rewritten parts of MS-DOS. For example, 3Com has a program called CIOSYS, which handles multiple disk I/O requests from different nodes on the network. The disadvantage is that it's not the standard MS-DOS that has been debugged by millions of users, but a quasi-version that may be used by only a few hundred or thousand people, and may still have its own unique problems or "bugs."

Hard-Disk Partition Size: Standard MS-DOS doesn't allow a disk to contain more than 32MB of data, even if the physical disk has a much larger capacity. In this case, the disk must be split into 32MB partitions in order to be used. This limitation can cause problems if you have files that contain many records. Some advanced versions of MS-DOS (such as Compaq DOS 3.31) allow partitions up to 512MB. If the network software does not support this option, you may still be limited to a maximum of 32MB.

Underutilization: With MS-DOS-based networks, the users' PCs can access the network devices that are set up to be shared, but this is not a reciprocal arrangement. For example, the backup devices and programs located on the network server cannot automatically access the hard drives on the individual PCs for regular backups. If someone is on vacation, their computer cannot be used for network offload processing. These limitations allow a large amount of processing power to go unused.

Install a PC LAN Using OS/2 Servers

OS/2 is the "big brother" to MS-DOS. It was designed for IBM by Microsoft as the next generation operating system for personal computers. OS/2 can be licensed from Microsoft, and most major hardware vendors already offer their own version compatible with IBM's, adapted and optimized for their own particular hardware.

OS/2 is still very new, but at some point DOS networks will seem hopelessly simple in comparison. With fewer than 10 percent of the 20 million PCs in the country converted, analysts and industry watchers predict that OS/2 will not become the dominant PC operating system for several years due to the increased costs involved with purchasing, installing and running it. OS/2 requires at least 2MB of memory to run effectively, and will not run on less than an AT class (80286) machine.

However, using OS/2 as the server operating system for a few selected workstations while continuing to use MS-DOS on the rest can give an organization a less expensive path to advanced capabilities, and allow a gradual upgrade to OS/2.

The operating system is only one piece of a network built on OS/2. Also required is the Microsoft LAN Manager, a separate program that allows information-sharing between PCs. Microsoft licenses the LAN Manager to various software and hardware companies, which in turn market their own products built around the LAN Manager.

Pros

An OS/2 network provides many advantages to the user who is willing and able to spend the additional money to get one up and running. Some of the advantages are as follows:

Multi-tasking: It's essential that you understand this critical feature. DOS is a *single-tasking* operating system, meaning that the operating system will perform one task to completion before allowing another task to be started. For example, if you were running Microsoft Word and wanted to get some information from your Lotus spreadsheet, you would have to exit Word, get the information, then re-execute Word to insert the spreadsheet data in your Word document.

With OS/2 you can perform several tasks simultaneously without exiting and re-entering each separate program. OS/2 can run multiple programs simultaneously, each program sharing the CPU, memory and other computer resources. For example, a large spreadsheet could be left to recalculate in the "background" away from the view of the user, while the user is preparing the main document on the screen in the foreground. The convenience and time-saving advantages of this capability are obvious.

As an example of multi-tasking versus single-tasking, suppose you have ten errands to run, and there are five people in your family. You could load the entire family in the car and do each errand one after the other until all were completed. This would be a single-tasking method. On the other hand, you could have each family member run two errands and report back. This would be multi-tasking or multiprocessing. The productivity and time savings are obvious.

Memory: DOS machines have been limited to 640K of main memory for applications usage. Various software and hardware workarounds have been invented to help deal with this, but 640K is the effective limit for the average user. OS/2 raises the memory limitation to a whopping (at least for right now) 16MB of memory. This enhanced memory will allow OS/2 to run several applications at once, and individual applications can be larger and more sophisticated.

DOS Compatibility: OS/2 allows MS-DOS programs to be executed, preserving the user's investment in DOS-based software. There are some limitations with this capability: any OS/2 processes running at the same time are stopped while the MS-DOS task is executed. Also, less memory is available for DOS applications on an OS/2-based system than on a DOS-based machine.

DOS–OS/2 Support: A network file server running OS/2, LAN Manager and networking software can support the central needs for both DOS and OS/2 workstations (not to mention Macintosh computers). This allows the gradual conversion of existing PCs to OS/2 with less pain and expense.

Advanced Software: OS/2 is spawning an entire generation of new applications software that takes advantage of these increased operating capabilities. The software that is developing most quickly is advanced database software such as the SQL server from Microsoft, Sybase and Ashton-Tate. This software will allow users far better control of data, increased performance and access to data from several workstation programs. For example, Microsoft Excel, dBASE IV and Microsoft Word might all be able to draw information out of the same SQL server database concurrently!

Uniform Interface: OS/2 applications are being developed with a *common graphical user interface* (GUI) called Presentation Manager (PM). Using a universal interface that behaves the same regardless of the application is a boon to productivity and the learning curve (ask any Macintosh owner!). Several companies have also announced versions of PM to run on other equipment, so interface across the organization will be uniform for end users of the system.

Long-Term Future: Many industry analysts predict that OS/2 will become the dominant PC operating system; it's only a question of when. If you're investing in a long-term solution and can afford it now, it may make sense to start with an OS/2 network rather than convert later.

Upward Integration: Hewlett-Packard (HP) and Digital Equipment Corporation (DEC) have announced support for the OS/2 LAN Manager. HP is developing software that will allow a Unix machine (see Implement a Unix-Based Solution in this chapter) to operate as an OS/2 server, and DEC is developing similar software that will allow a DEC VAX to do the same. Once completed, this capability will give the OS/2 network the ability to handle very large database and processing-intensive tasks if necessary.

This isn't to say that OS/2 is a perfect solution; there are disadvantages that should be discussed, some of which have already been mentioned, including additional hardware costs and more expensive software costs. Others come to mind:

Cons

Complexity: OS/2 has many of the features of a minicomputer operating system—security, resource sharing, multi-tasking and audit trails (see Buy a Minicomputer in this chapter). But with these enhancements come the complexity of installation and management. Without attention to these areas, many of the benefits of OS/2 will go unrealized. A dedicated system administrator or consultant may be required to manage OS/2.

Cost: The cost of installing an OS/2 network is significantly higher than a DOS-based network, since faster machines (386 and up) are required, as well as additional memory per machine, more expensive software and more intensive user training.

Limited Software: Although the number of OS/2-compatible software products is growing by leaps and bounds, they don't begin to equal the width (number of applications) and breadth (number of successful users) of DOS applications. Most of the applications to date have been conversions from DOS-based systems and have not taken advantage of the newer features of OS/2.

Immaturity: OS/2 is still young compared to all other accepted operating systems. It does have bugs; it's optimized for the 80286 processor, which has already been superseded by the 80386.

As more advanced server software is developed and additional applications are built to take advantage of OS/2, the capabilities will far exceed those of MS-DOS, with both stand-alone and networked solutions. The real question is, When is this going to happen? Network software producers are providing a smooth upgrade path for organizations that have existing DOS LANs, so conversion should not be a major problem for most organizations.

Implement a Unix-Based Solution

Unix is an operating system developed by AT&T at Bell Labs in the early Seventies. Unix offers all the benefits of a traditional minicomputer operating system, but with a unique twist: it's able to run on virtually any type of computer, offering unparalleled transportability among manufacturers of hardware.

Over the years, Unix has been both praised and panned. Enthusiasts insisted that Unix would eclipse all other operating systems and become world-dominant, while detractors were sure it would die a slow and lingering death.

Today, Unix runs on a large number of computers and is indeed becoming much more of a standard than many of the doubters imagined. There are still issues to be resolved. For example, Unix comes in several different "flavors," making it somewhat incompatible across these various versions. On the low end, Xenix (a version of Unix developed by Microsoft) has a large number of installations. Xenix runs on Intel-based computers, 286- and 386-based, giving low-cost entry into the multi-user Unix marketplace. Unix System V is the standard AT&T version of Unix, and the University of California at Berkeley came out with its own version that was quickly adopted by companies such as Sun Microsystems (known as Berkeley Unix). In 1988, AT&T purchased a substantial portion of Sun Microsystems, and a combined version of Unix is expected to be the eventual result of their joint effort.

An increasing amount of end-user software is being developed for the Unix environment and Unix has very strong networking capabilities built into the operating system. Many companies use a Unix-based computer as a central communications processor because of its flexibility in communicating with most types of proprietary equipment. Some PC software vendors, including Lotus and Ashton-Tate, have announced future Unix support of their products as well.

If your organization demands a very flexible systems architecture for disparate users and a wide range of computers, Unix deserves a serious look. One advantage of Unix is its ability to run on a machine as small as an IBM AT or as large as a mainframe capable of handling hundreds of users concurrently.

Unix is also forging alliances with OS/2. Hewlett-Packard is writing an interface for Unix to allow a Unix-based machine to act as a server on an OS/2 network. Unix, DOS and OS/2 are the major "open" operating environments, and will merge together over time.

Pros

Flexibility: If your organization is small, you can purchase Unix software that will run on a small, five-user system at very competitive prices. If in a few years your company needs a computer system that can handle 100 users concurrently, chances are good that the same software you started with can be moved to the larger system. This is especially true if you plan for growth.

Software Availability: Many of the PC market leaders now have ported their products to Unix systems. Packages available now include WordPerfect, AutoCAD, FoxBASE, and many other vendors are in the process of offering Unix versions as well.

Central Processing: Like the traditional mini, users of the Unix system share the central processor to accomplish tasks. This can allow the network administrator to create a simple and easy-to-learn "shell" for network users, who may never know that they're using the Unix operating system.

Easy Networking: One of the best built-in features of Unix is its ability to network with other computers running Unix and many computers that aren't running Unix. File transfer, remote log-in and intermachine communication can be easily accomplished.

DOS and OS/2 Integration: Several vendors, including Hewlett-Packard, are working feverishly to allow mixing OS/2 networks, DOS workstations and Unix minicomputers in a transparent environment that will give the end user the best of each environment without the limitations associated with mixing operating systems. This trio will assume an increasing role in most large organizations that need more than DOS and OS/2 to function. Presentation Manager and other graphical interfaces will at some point shield the end user from the complexities of the system.

Cons

Complexity: Unix is a complex operating system and demands a higher level of support and sophistication. However, turnkey solutions from vendors for a specific application can be relatively trouble-free and easy to use.

Unfamiliarity: Because most end users aren't familiar with Unix, there can be a learning curve for those users who want to develop an understanding of the capabilities of the operating system.

Incompatibility: Until the various versions of Unix blend together, there will be confusion over which is better. The software you want to use may not be ported to your particular version of Unix. This should work itself out over time; but if your needs are immediate, this can be a real stumbling block.

How Can Your Organization Evaluate Unix?

Evaluating Unix is difficult, since far fewer retail computer dealers sell Unix-based boxes (although this is changing quickly). One of the best ways to evaluate it is to contact the hardware manufacturers directly and ask for information on Value Added Resellers (VARs) in your area. Ask the VAR for customer references; you may be surprised to find many companies running Unix-based solutions very effectively. If you see this in action, you can pursue a solution through the VAR recommended by the hardware manufacturer.

If you're interested in learning more about Unix, some valuable books and magazines that will help you on your way are listed in the appendix of this book.

Implement a Macintosh Solution

When first released, the Apple Macintosh wasn't regarded as a serious business computer. Its radically different approach—using icons and a mouse along with a user-friendly interface—was looked upon as foreign and unusual by millions of PC users.

Since that time, Mac has made tremendous inroads into the business community, initially in the desktop publishing area, but now in almost every area within organizations. Market-leading software from the MS-DOS world has been moved to the Mac, allowing non-Mac users an easy transition. Examples of this are dBASE and its compatibles, AutoCAD, and Microsoft Word. Packages developed exclusively for the Mac are being moved to the PC; a prime example of this is Microsoft Excel.

The Macintosh comes with built-in networking capabilities using a technology called AppleTalk. Cables can be run from one machine to another, giving device- and file-sharing capabilities. Macs can also be attached to an increasing number of MS-DOS networks, allowing a mixture of PCs and Macs to be used on the same network.

TOPS, a Sun Microsystems company located in Berkeley, CA, also supplies a popular networking solution for the Macintosh, allowing file transfer with a number of machines including Sun's Unix workstations and IBM PCs.

My opinion is that the Mac is a very good machine and bears investigation. I do not feel that an all-Mac solution for a large number of users is optimal except under special circumstances that are beyond the scope of this book. (For an excellent book that covers Macintosh networking strategies, see the bibliography.)

Since the Mac has already penetrated many organizations and seems to be there to stay, this is one area where a hybrid solution will make sense for many organizations. PC network vendors such as 3Com and Novell offer solutions that allow the Mac to plug into a PC network for electronic mail, file-sharing and printer services.

Build a Hybrid Solution

A hybrid solution is made of pieces from each of the above solutions. If done correctly, a hybrid can incorporate most of the advantages and minimize the disadvantages of each solution. However, if you create a hybrid solution (or pay someone good money to do it for you) and it's built incorrectly, you can wind up with an even bigger mess to clean up than if you had stuck with a simple, single-architecture strategy.

Unix, OS/2 and DOS are all growing together at a rapid pace. I would estimate that by 1992, there will be computer environments that look so similar the end users won't know which background operating system is being used. Computers may never be as simple to use as the telephone, but eventually most computers should at least have a common, intuitive method for getting basic tasks done. It seems like that day is finally drawing near.

Many larger organizations have developed hybrid networks simply because they started with multiple technologies before networking. As technology developed, these "islands of automation" grew network "roots" and began to become interconnected. There are few systems today that cannot be connected to a network that will allow information transfer; the hardware companies have made tremendous progress in designing their machines to connect to others.

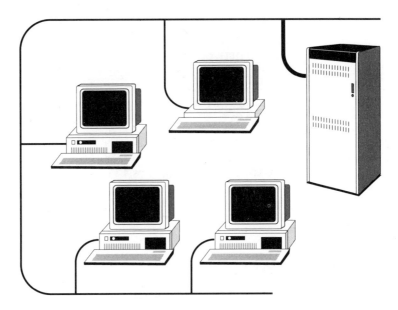

Figure 4.1   Hybrid solution: combining personal computers and a mini.

When I worked for DEC in 1982, its PDP and VAX machines could barely talk to each other—and they were produced by the same manufacturer. The thought of tying them into other computers (someone had an Apple II at the facility) was not even considered.

One type of hybrid system found in many larger companies is the combination of personal computers and a departmental minicomputer. The minicomputer is used for shared applications such as order processing or inventory control; the personal computers act as terminals, using terminal emulation software. When not being used to access the minicomputer, the personal computers can be used to run Lotus 1-2-3 or other PC-oriented applications. Information can be exchanged between the mini and the personal computers, and electronic mail may reside on either or both systems.

This setup gives the user the best of both strategies, as well as increasing the software base from which to choose. It also costs more than either single solution, and demands more support time and expertise. Intermachine networking can be difficult, but most vendors are working hard to provide easy access to their systems.

If possible, avoid having several types of PC networks in the same company. While minicomputer and mainframe vendors have forged links between major systems, communication between PC LANs can be difficult and maintenance-intensive. For example, there are few solutions for connecting a Novell network with a 3Com network, or a Novell network with an AT&T StarLan network. If the organization is split, having a standard type of network is preferable to trying to connect them later. Communications links undoubtedly will be invented, but avoiding this problem is the easiest way to eliminate headaches.

If your organization has installed a hybrid solution, chances are good that you have a dedicated support staff to handle the hardware and software. As time continues, management should work with the support staff to ensure that the technical strategy is in tune with the business goals of the organization.

Buy a Minicomputer

Purchasing a minicomputer has been the traditional way for a department or company to accomplish large amounts of computer processing and sharing of information among many individuals within the organization. Vendors such as DEC, Prime, Wang and Data General all have various solutions aimed at handling the information-sharing needs of five or more users. Digital in particular has been successful with its VAX line of minicomputers. The VAX line starts with a one- to two-user system that can expand to allow thousands of people to share the same information without changing the software used. Here are some of the advantages of purchasing a minicomputer:

Pros

User Simplicity: In its simplest form, a minicomputer consists of a central computer with two or more computer terminals attached. These are typically "dumb" terminals that have no computer CPU built into them. The terminals rely on the central minicomputer for all processing of information. The user's screen and keyboard are simple to work with, so training time is reduced. If desired, the vendor can provide all support functions, including technical system management, software installation and reconfiguration when any additional equipment is purchased.

Sharing Resources: The minicomputer shares its processing power among everyone using it by means of a "multi-user/multi-tasking" operating system. This is an effective way to utilize the CPU, the disk drives and other devices that may be attached to the minicomputer. In a PC environment under MS-DOS, if a station isn't in use, its processing power is unavailable to any other user within the organization. Minicomputer operating systems, in contrast, are designed to handle many users without appreciable degradation of performance, allowing each user to feel he or she has exclusive access to the computer.

Applications Software: A wide base of seasoned applications software is available for minicomputers. By "seasoned" I mean that the software company can cite people and organizations who have used their software successfully for several years with very few problems. Most PC software in the multiple-user environment is still relatively new and evolving rapidly, so the chance for bugs in the software is high, and the number of established users is usually small. There are some notable exceptions to this: software development in the PC environment is making great strides in terms of user interface, interaction with databases and other advanced features.

Security: Security systems built into the minicomputer's operating system are typically more advanced than the ones available on today's DOS-based networks. A terminal-based system limits access of unauthorized individuals to corporate information. Because there's no storage unit on the terminal, it's not possible for someone to make a floppy disk of your customer file and remove it from the premises. These safeguards are important in protecting information from exposure to those who aren't designated to see it.

Central Control: A minicomputer demands supervision by someone who is experienced in its operation; the average department user will not be able to assume the duties of managing the computer simply by reading the manual or attending a one-day training class. This necessitates central control, typically a part-time or full-time system administrator, for managing the system. Proper management is especially important in keeping all information stored on the system copied to tape and backed up regularly. Having a central location makes it more convenient to back up and maintain the information in the event of a problem.

Growth Options: If your organization is growing rapidly, minicomputers can be easily expanded or upgraded to handle more end users or additional processing tasks. This can be done by switching hardware and moving the existing software to a larger computer furnished by the minicomputer vendor.

An example is Microsoft, the largest PC software company in the country. In 1983 it purchased a VAX minicomputer and applications software packages to handle order management, production, purchasing and accounting. This single computer was designed to accommodate 30 people. As the company grew, additional users were added to the system at a very rapid pace. Today the system has been expanded to include five large VAX computers with shared disk drives and printers. It can accommodate hundreds of users at the same time, and the applications software didn't require rewriting each time a new piece of equipment was added or upgraded.

Batch Processing Capability: Minicomputers offer the capability known as batch processing. This allows for processing to be done in an unattended mode, which is especially effective for utilizing the computer at night and on weekends.

For example, a company may want to recalculate its projected inventory requirements for the next 12 months. Rather than do this during the workday, utilizing resources that someone else could be using for electronic mail or word processing, the inventory report could be set up or "submitted" to run at night. This ensures that the data will be in a nonchanging or "quiet" state, and the recalculation will not deprive daytime users of their machine.

Remote Access: Using dial-up or dedicated telephone circuits, users can easily access a minicomputer from remote locations, normally with very good response time and full functionality, since all processing is done on the central processor. This capability can allow a large number of distributed users easy access to information.

Vendor Support: Most minicomputer vendors have full-scope support contracts available, covering any hardware, peripheral equipment and software purchased from the vendor. In the event of a problem, only one phone call is necessary to arrange for prompt and convenient scheduling for service.

These advantages make an impressive list. Minis have done extremely well over the years; many very large companies use them in lieu of a corporate mainframe computer. There are many examples of successful, large-scale, minicomputer-based information systems. However, as with any solution, this one has some disadvantages.

Cons

Cost: The cost per user on a minicomputer-based system is generally higher than on a PC-based solution. Vendors will argue this in any number of ways, but I think this is a fair statement in the majority of cases. In addition, expenditures for a minicomputer must be made in one large chunk, which could be a heavy burden for a growing business already cramped by cash flow.

Software: The vast amounts of software available on the PC are not available on minicomputers. If a particular piece of software *is* available, the cost is usually higher. For example, while there are packages that can read files generated from Lotus 1-2-3, there isn't a version of 1-2-3 from Lotus available for a VAX or IBM minicomputer (one should be available soon). Also, some packages become much more expensive when purchased for a minicomputer rather than for a PC.

Degradation/Capacity: The minicomputer works on the principle of sharing a central computing "brain" (the CPU). When one person uses the computer, that person has access to 100 percent of the computer's capacity. When four people use that computer, they each receive a 25 percent share (this is much more complicated in reality, but we'll keep it simple for purposes of discussion). As more people use the computer at one time, the amount of resources available to each user decreases. This means that each person's tasks take longer, which can be especially inconvenient during periods of peak activity when everyone needs better response time. Additional capacity can be added, but that usually involves large capital outlays.

Single Point of Failure: If all your data are in one box (the minicomputer) and the computer goes down, everyone waits until it's fixed. Some minicomputer vendors provide capabilities for fault tolerance or equipment that will continue to work even if some parts fail, but this is expensive and beyond the scope of most organizations in terms of cost and management.

Complexity of Operation: Depending on your organization, you will probably need to designate at least one person to operate and maintain the minicomputer. These duties would include adding new accounts, tuning the system for optimum performance, rearranging disk space and other items that need to be taken care of. Problems created through poor operation affect everyone using the system. In brief, a minicomputer system usually requires more maintenance and expertise than a PC-based system.

Obsolescence: The pace for producing faster and higher capacity hardware has greatly accelerated over the past ten years, causing many minicomputers to become obsolete before they're paid for! A few short years ago (1983), an organization I worked for purchased an advanced VAX minicomputer for $180,000. Today (1989), the market value of that system is only around $20,000 due to the even more advanced CPUs that have been released by DEC, Sun Microsystems and other companies.

Deciding Factors

As the White Rabbit said to Alice, if you don't know where you're going, it doesn't matter which path you take. The same is true in computer networking: If you don't know where you want to end up, there are many ways to get there.

Because there are so many good ones, in many cases it's difficult to choose the correct solution. Here are some factors that can push the decision one way or the other, depending on the specific needs of your organization:

Distributed Processing: If all the users within your organization need to have fast and accurate access to the same database, and the organization is spread across the country or the world, the minicomputer is still the leader in this capability. Until advances are made in network database and communications software, this won't change significantly.

Fault Tolerance/Nonstop Processing: The minicomputer world has more solutions in place right now, but the networks are gaining fast. Of course, if you're using a network and it goes down, you still have your local PC and software, which can be set up to perform most tasks individually.

Quick Growth and Flexibility: LANs are hard to beat in this category. New processing can be integrated while the network is up, equipment is immediately available, and if necessary the entire network can be picked up and moved.

Security: For those applications where security is a top priority, the sophisticated operating systems of minicomputers currently have the edge over LANs.

Cost: Because of the modular nature of LANs, costs can be spread out over a longer period of time, with capacity added as you need it, not in large, expensive upgrades to a central processor.

So Which Way to Go?

It would be wonderful if the answer was the same for all organizations worldwide. Unfortunately, the best solution can be determined only by a thorough analysis of what your organization needs to accomplish, the time frame, and the available funds. When you factor in changing technology, you have a complex set of choices for accomplishing the organization's goals.

As a starting point, use the following outline and charts from Chapter 3. Although they won't provide all the answers you need to chart your course, they'll help you get started. The following are some general directions to consider about the course of the next few years of technology and how it could affect your organization:

Playing the Waiting Game

Wait, if . . .

- You aren't sure what to do.
- Your business is stable, predictable and doing well.
- Some small, easy steps will provide significant bottom-line improvement.
- A viable solution to your needs cannot be demonstrated.
- Other organizational issues need addressing to prepare for automation.

Don't wait, if . . .

- Waiting is simply a way to avoid the inevitable.
- The demands on your organization are increasing dramatically.
- A new system will spell the difference between succeeding and failing.
- Even a mediocre solution will provide big benefits.
- You're looking for the perfect solution (there's no such thing).

DOS-based Network

Use a DOS-based network, when . . .

- You need a network solution now.
- You already have an installed base of PCs.
- The solution you need will run on a DOS-based network.
- You want to use primarily DOS-based applications software.
- You may want to grow into an OS/2 solution.
- The lowest cost for multi-user access is desired.

Don't use a DOS-based network, when . . .

- Current or expected processing load exceeds capacity of networked PCs.
- Your application demands large amounts of dial-in, remote access.
- A simpler solution will solve the long-term problem.

OS/2 Network

Use an OS/2 network, when . . .

- The processing capabilities of a DOS LAN are exceeded.
- The network is being installed to reap benefits more than 12 months out.
- Extra workstation, server and software costs aren't an issue.

Don't use an OS/2 network, when . . .

- Most of your important applications are still MS-DOS-based.
- You need an installed, working and mature system quickly.
- You're counting on software not yet delivered to the market.
- You want the most inexpensive solution.

Unix System

Use a Unix system, when . . .

- Ultimate hardware and software flexibility is desired.
- You want to unify already existing hardware.

- Most tasks require a high-performance workstation.
- You don't want to change software again.
- You need PC prices now, mini capacity later.

Macintosh

Use a Macintosh system, when . . .

- Your people already know the Mac.
- The software you need runs only on the Mac platform.
- Ease of use is the overriding concern.

Don't use a Macintosh, when . . .

- You want to upgrade the same software to a bigger machine.
- Heavy multi-user database processing is a critical requirement.
- You want easy integration with other devices.
- You want compatibility among equipment from several manufacturers.

Hybrid Solution

Implement a hybrid system, when . . .

- You already have a mixture of equipment.
- A single type of computer architecture won't solve your requirements effectively.
- You want different control points (i.e., MIS controls the mainframe, individual divisions control the mini, departments control the LAN).

Don't install a hybrid system, when . . .

- You want to minimize technical support.
- You want to minimize the number of vendors.
- A single hardware/software answer will accomplish your needs.

Minicomputer-Only Solution

Purchase a minicomputer, if . . .

- High-speed, distributed remote access is needed.
- Large amounts of batch/off-line processing are required.
- The multi-user cooperative workload can't be handled by a PC network.
- Centralized security is a must.
- A single, all-encompassing vendor is desired.
- The absolute best solution is available only with a minicomputer.

Don't purchase a minicomputer, if...

- Individual projects and applications account for most of the workload.
- The workload can easily be handled by a PC network.
- Users are already productive with PCs.
- Costs exceed equivalent PC solutions.

Keep It as Simple as Possible

With technology growing at such a rapid pace, it's easy for an organization to get overrun with solutions. One department uses Macs, another builds a PC network, another implements a Unix solution, and the MIS department clings to the previous generation of minicomputer or mainframe. This diversity and haphazard growth can cause tremendous trauma in the organization later on.

Many times, management gives a helping hand to the confusion, viewing it as departmental independence. The same management would think it crazy if each department purchased its own telephone system that could not contact the remainder of the organization. Find a solution that works and avoid dabbling in every available option. Some things won't get done in an optimum way, but the right choice will ensure that the most "bang for the buck" is obtained throughout the organization.

Focus on Results

As we discussed earlier, all of the technology injected into an organization should be focused on making the company more effective, thus producing greater profits. If that doesn't happen, re-deploy the technology where it will produce these desired results.

Too many unused personal computers are gathering dust on managers' desks, in offices or in stockrooms. Get involved in measuring the effective use of these devices and see what they're worth. If they're not working to your satisfaction, sell them and use the money for something that does get results.

Look to the Long-Term Standards

The items you're purchasing will be around for a long time. Putting the time in up front to make the best decision is important; it will minimize the amount of equipment, software and effort wasted. Buy items that are in the mainstream if you want to maximize the life of your investments; the larger the installed base of the particular piece of hardware or software, the greater the chance someone will find a way to make it last longer and give it greater functionality. MS-DOS and Unix are existing standards, with OS/2 making a bid to become the next standard operating system. In a few years, small to medium-size organizations may need little else to solve their information processing objectives.

Moving On

The next chapter deals with some short-term connectivity solutions that your organization can use regardless of whether a decision has been made on acquiring a more advanced solution. If a solution for the longer term is acquired, with very little cost or effort the technologies described in the next chapter can either be incorporated or shifted to another part of the organization.

5

Short-Term Alternatives

If by now you've decided you don't need a full-blown LAN, this chapter will be especially useful. You'll learn the facts about alternatives that allow information exchange and device-sharing without the costs of a full-blown network.

Even if you do plan to install a network, the following factors may require that you use short-term solutions in the interim.

Cost Constraints: If you don't have a lot of money, most short-term solutions are inexpensive when compared to installing a fully functional network.

Simplicity: If you're trying to solve a simple problem, the best solution may be simple as well.

Geography: Offices of your company may be too far apart to take advantage of LAN facilities and connections. Remote sales offices, warehouse space or other facilities may require simple rather than full solutions.

Timing/Expediency: You might need some immediate solutions while installing a larger network, to provide relief during a protracted implementation period.

Security: You may not want certain information exposed on your LAN, or you may require an additional layer of backup data.

If you decide to utilize some of these alternatives, please heed the following suggestions:

Choose Brand Names: Before buying, do some research to find out who makes a high-quality component. You can purchase printer switches at any flea market, but it pays to know which ones have a reputation for working well, with all the expected features. Many computer periodicals and books review hardware and software.

Listen to Others: Someone who has used a specific technology can be an invaluable source of information. If he or she has used it successfully for several weeks or months, chances are good it will work for you. He or she can also lead you to professionals who support the product or offer similar solutions.

Write a Procedure: If you set up something that's complex, write a simple procedure to cover its operation and post it near the device. This will help everyone who uses it to understand how it operates and how to deal with problems that might arise. What's more frustrating than to be on vacation and have someone track you down because a printer-sharing device won't work!

Monitor Usage/Reevaluate: New technology should help, not hinder, and the true test for this is usage. After your equipment has been installed for a while, monitor whether it's being used and how well it's working. I have seen companies install new technology and, predictably, everyone promptly ignored the new, improved system and continued to do things the old way.

Teach Your Staff: Often, the reason a system goes unused is because of a lack of training. Whenever the budget allows, plan to train key employees on new technologies, with seminars and workshops, books and periodicals or on-site tutorials. If the budget doesn't allow, find a way to get your staff trained anyway.

Stay Ahead of the Curve: Frequently re-evaluate capacity and long-term usefulness of short-term solutions. You may need something more functional as usage expands, and you don't want to get caught short at a critical time.

Now that we've noted some advantages and pitfalls, let's examine two benefits that a full network provides without using a network—*information exchange* (file transfer) and *peripheral device sharing*.

Information Exchange

Floppy Disks

Almost all personal computers come equipped with one or two floppy disk drives. These drives, and the corresponding disks, come in two sizes—5 1/4 inches and 3 1/2 inches. The 3 1/2-inch floppy is enclosed in a hard plastic case, while the 5 1/4-inch size is soft and flexible. The 5 1/4-inch disks, depending on their capacity, can hold

360K or 1.2 megabytes (MB) of data. (K equals 1,024 characters; MB equals 1,024 K.) The 3 1/2-inch drives typically hold 720K although a higher capacity (1.44MB) is supported on some machines.

The floppy disk is the most common method of transferring information among PCs. Using various software written to enhance their capabilities, floppies can transfer large amounts of information accurately. Following are the major advantages and disadvantages of floppy disks.

Advantages

Universality: Since most personal computers have floppy disk drives, there's a good chance that you can transfer information in this manner. Most software packages for personal computers are distributed on floppy disk for this reason.

Cost: Floppy disks are inexpensive, particularly when the amount of information to be transferred or stored is small. If you routinely use 60 large-capacity floppy disks for backup, there is probably a more effective method; but for casual information transfer and storage, the economics of floppy disks are hard to beat.

Software Enhancements: Software has been developed for floppy disks that allows them to hold larger amounts of information by compressing the data files, and to store large files by breaking them into pieces that can fit on sets of floppy disks.

Disadvantages

Speed: It takes a relatively long time to copy a large file to a floppy disk, move it to another machine and copy it off. It takes much longer for the floppy disk to pass information to the computer it is installed within, in comparison to the speed of a hard disk.

Capacity: It doesn't take a lot of information to exceed the capacity of one disk, particularly when CAD, desktop publishing and other complex files are involved. Special utilities software is usually required to copy files larger than the size of the floppy. Even with the software, copying a file that requires 20 floppy disk swaps isn't the best way to approach the problem (unless you have to do it only once a year, in which case it probably isn't worth buying additional equipment).

Incompatibility: As the various standards for floppy disk size and capacity have evolved, it's become harder to ensure that the disks you produce can be read by every machine they're transferred to. For example, a 360K drive on an IBM XT will not be able to read a high-capacity 1.2MB floppy generated on a Compaq 386. With the introduction of the newer 3 1/2-inch drive, the situation has become even more complex.

Fragility: Floppy disks are easily damaged, particularly the older 5 1/4-inch media, which are protected only by a thin, flexible sheath and sleeve. The readable part of the disk is exposed as well. Heat, dirt and rough handling can cause damage to the floppy, rendering its contents useless. The newer 3 1/2-inch format is more durable, with its hard plastic shell and a fold-back protector covering the disk when it's not in use.

Removable High-Capacity Disks

One of the earliest methods of reliably and quickly transferring a lot of information among personal computers was the Bernoulli Box, manufactured by IOMEGA Corporation. The Bernoulli Box is an external device, attached to the computer via a cable and a controller card installed in an expansion slot within the computer. Software loaded in the personal computer's start-up programs allows it to recognize the information stored on the device.

The disks or cartridges used with the Bernoulli Box are removable and can be transferred to another Bernoulli Box on a separate computer. The disk cartridges can hold large amounts of information (10- and 20-megabyte models are traditional sizes), and the access speeds are very fast, in some cases rivaling or exceeding the speed of the hard-disk units within the PC. Using additional cartridges, which are reasonably inexpensive ($50 to $60 each), provides the capability for separating the data (e.g., one cartridge per project or department) and for "locking up" sensitive data. Many other vendors have come out with similar systems that offer additional storage capability, speed and other features.

Cartridge Tape Backup Units (Internal and External)

Cartridge tape drives have been available for personal computers for quite a while; they provide an excellent method of backing up or archiving the personal computer's hard-disk storage unit.

As a means of sharing information among computers, tape units haven't been universally compatible among manufacturers. This can be a problem unless one specific type of tape is purchased for each personal computer within the organization. If this is done, the cartridge tape can be an excellent method for storing information and transferring large amounts of data to other computers.

For example, an organization that owns six Compaq Deskpro computers, each equipped with a Compaq tape drive, can easily and inexpensively share information and a common backup method. Quality devices range in price from $250 to more than $5,000. On the low end of the scale is an external 40MB tape unit. On the high end is a tape technology called helical scan, which uses inexpensive 8mm tapes and can store an amazing 2.2 gigabytes of information on a single tape.

Another strategy used in conjunction with cartridge tape units is to install a tape unit controller card to each PC and use one portable external tape backup unit. This lets all machines share the device, reducing the capital outlays required for each computer to have its own unit. The controller cards aren't expensive ($100 to $150), and the typical tape device isn't heavily used.

If necessary, multiple tape units can be purchased, further ensuring that one is always available and in working order. High-quality tapes should be purchased and the backup units should be maintained in accordance with the manufacturer's guidelines.

Note: Conduct periodic tests of your backups to ensure that the technology is working as it should. There is no worse time than when a crisis arrives to find out the backup unit is malfunctioning or that the tapes are blank due to improper software commands.

Optical Disk Units

The optical disk is a fairly new product in the PC marketplace. These devices, which store information on platters similar to a stereo's compact disk, can hold tremendous amounts of information at a relatively low price. A typical unit might hold 800 megabytes of data on one removable cartridge, the equivalent of 2,200 360K floppy disks! Costs range from $3,000 to $7,000, with cartridges costing $50 to $150 each, depending upon capacity. I've been using an 800-megabyte unit, and it's worked flawlessly so far.

If the unit is a WORM (write once, read many times) technology drive, data can be stored indelibly, with no chance of overwriting or erasing the contents of the disk. This scenario is ideal for historical archives (accounting records, documents, drawings). Like tape drives, multiple controller cards can be purchased, allowing you to move the optical disk unit among several personal computers.

This technology can also allow you to keep a master copy of all your data off-site from your organization. In case of a disaster (fire, flood, vandalism), you would be able to reconstruct your information. Access time is currently slow for copying and retrieving information (100 milliseconds compared to 15 to 40 milliseconds for a fast hard disk), but some manufacturers are expected to announce drives that will rival the access speeds of hard disks. Also under development is the capability to erase and re-use the optical surface.

Serial Transfer Units

Transferring data among computers can be done directly through the use of a cable and software. The cable is attached to the serial port of each computer, and the software enables the computers to copy files from one to the other. A product that accomplishes this task at a reasonable cost is LapLink from Traveling Software in Bothell, WA.

This innovative product allows two PCs to share files directly. The product consists of a multihead cable which can connect either size serial port (25-pin or 9-pin) on the two machines, or use the two parallel ports (for an even faster connection) and some software that allows each machine access to the other's hard disk.

As an example, I took a Compaq SLT portable on a recent trip. I wanted to do some work on this book while I was on the road. I had never used this product previously, but within 15 minutes I had hooked it up, transferred the necessary files from my home machine to the portable—without messy disk transfers and a trip to another machine that could read both 5 1/4-inch and 3 1/2-inch disks. The instructions were easy to understand, the software made sense without the instructions, and the price was right (around $100). If I wanted to duplicate just that functionality with a LAN, it would have cost substantially more money.

Modems/Telephone Lines

Computer modems can be used to access and transfer information among personal computers, and are particularly useful when the machines are too far apart to be joined by a simple cable. A modem is attached to each personal computer and a phone line is provided for each. The software allows one personal computer to call the other and exchange information.

One package I've used is PC Anywhere, and it worked well for file transfer and remote access. The required software costs around $100. As this book goes to press, 2400-baud modems cost around $150 each, so the total solution would be approximately $200 per PC.

Device-Sharing

A full-fledged PC network will facilitate the sharing of common devices, such as printers, among several users. However, there are many alternatives that can provide this capability inexpensively and with less complexity.

The A/B Switch Box

One of the least expensive ways for two personal computers to share a common printer is the A/B switch. This device can cost from $15 to $100. It provides ports for the printer on one side of the box and two PC printer cables on the other side. The user must manually switch the box so that his or her cable letter is connected to the printer cable.

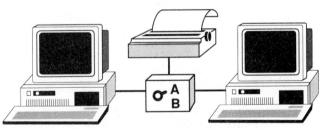

Figure 5.1   A/B switch box: sharing resources efficiently.

This is a simple, manual connection device that's easy to implement and use, and there's no software cost or complexity involved. This device is designed to provide more people with access to a printer: but because it's a manual process, frequent users may find this method frustrating, particularly if the printer switch is across the room or down the hall.

Intelligent Switching Systems

A more functional implementation of the A/B box is an intelligent or automatic printer switch. This device takes over the switching portion of the A/B box. It electronically senses who wants to use the printer, makes the proper connection and waits for the next printer request. These devices allow a larger number of printers and personal computers to be connected without the inconvenience of a manual switching system. They're more expensive than a manual system but still much less than a LAN.

Intelligent switch boxes range in price from $150 to more than $1,000. Some models come with special software that will allow file transfer and primitive messaging as well. Others come with the ability to daisy-chain the boxes, allowing a number of users to access a number of devices.

Some automatic switch boxes offer print buffers that store print jobs in memory if the user cannot access the printer because another job is in progress. When the first job is complete, the switch automatically prints the second job.

Zero-Slot LANs

If you have looked at the alternatives mentioned and decided that you want to share both information *and* devices, but still don't want to get into an expensive network solution, several vendors offer "mini" networks, or *zero-slot LANs*.

The term zero slot means that no traditional network card has to be installed within the PC. Instead, the serial port on the existing computer is used as the connector to other computers and printers.

This type of system offers an inexpensive solution to networking (from $100 to $300 per PC), but some limitations exist:

Growth: A zero-slot LAN isn't designed to handle traffic between a large number of computers. A typical limitation is eight computers before some type of device is needed to extend the network to another eight computers. If your company expects significant growth, this type of limitation can become critical at exactly the wrong moment—when the network has become successful and everyone wants to use it!

Data-sharing: Information-sharing on a serial port network is typically done on a file-by-file basis. This limits or prohibits the interactive use of database files. For example, each user could exchange copies of Lotus 1-2-3 files, but only one user at a time could access the customer master file for an inquiry. In many environments, this might be an unacceptable solution.

Speed: The speed of this type of network is limited by the serial port hardware on the individual workstations, which is around 115KB, or .1 megabytes per second. This is substantially slower than the speeds full-fledged networks offer.

If your business isn't growing rapidly in terms of data-sharing or printer use, these low-end networks can represent an excellent value. They can also be an interim solution when an organization is unsure of its strategy or needs. Because of the low cost, this kind of network can be a throw-away or possibly a hand-me-down item: when one department moves up to a full-fledged network, another area of the organization can absorb this partial solution.

Low-Cost Peer-to-Peer Networks

One step above zero-slot LANs, but still below the capability of a full network, are the *peer-to-peer* networking solutions. These systems are less expensive to install and maintain. They offer the file-sharing, file-transfer and printer-sharing capabilities of full-fledged LANs, but are slower and less expandable.

This type of network does not use a central file server. Rather, each machine on the network can be set to be a resource shared by others on the same network. The other machines on the network can access files on the hard disk of the "superstation," as well as using the printers attached to it for shared printing.

One vendor who produces such a solution is Artisoft (Tucson, AZ); the product is called LANtastic. This innovative system uses only 10K to 20K of memory on the workstations and 40K to 50K on the station that also acts as the server. It can transfer data at the respectable speed of 2MB per second, and has a per-station cost of under $200. Most multi-user applications software will run very well (but check them before buying).

The disadvantages of such a solution are similar to those of zero-slot LANs—limited growth potential and lack of connectivity to other vendors' networks. For a small company that plans to remain small, however, this type of solution can be an excellent alternative—a way to tiptoe into a full-blown network.

Moving On

As you've seen, there's an extensive selection of devices that can provide many of the functions of a full-fledged LAN without large investments of capital or time. As you consider the options, keep the following guidelines in mind:

Purchasing a workable short-term solution is not just economical, it's also good business. Why use a bulldozer when all you really need is a shovel? Money spent on technology should generate revenue, not take it away.

Information exchange can be done in a variety of ways; choose the way that works best for your application and budget. Be alert for decreasing productivity and increasing frustration—the best indicators that you're outgrowing your present strategies.

If data-sharing is not an important item for your organization, consider a simpler and less expensive (though less efficient) sub-LAN or zero-slot LAN.

Optical disks represent one of the best methods for off-site backup and archiving. They can hold a lot of data in a small space, and because the medium is unerasable, the archives are permanent.

If you've come this far and still haven't solved your problems, you need either a LAN or a more advanced solution. Before we begin to explore fully functional LANs, let's take a look at applications software, the guiding force behind any network.

6

Applications Software–the Guiding Force

Applications software is the most visible and important aspect of computers, whether they're networked or stand-alone. It's what the average user works with every day. Whether it's Microsoft Word, WordPerfect, Lotus 1-2-3, dBASE, AutoCAD or SBT's Accounting Library, these programs are responsible for the rapid growth of personal and networked computer usage.

I've heard software described as "the tail that wags the dog," and it's an apt description. Picking the right software for stand-alone and networked computers is very important to an organization. Standardizing can increase productivity and decrease training and learning time. Using industry-standard software also cuts down on the amount of research required and provides a ready-made support network for training employees.

Many readers won't remember the drudgery of maintaining manual card files or producing financial summaries by hand. How many people do you know who still use a typewriter and carbon paper for document processing? How many large, handwritten spreadsheets have crossed your desk lately? Since VisiCalc emerged as the first widely used spreadsheet, people have flocked to computer stores in search of software that can handle the tedious tasks that used to be done manually.

What Are You Using Now?

Take a look at the applications software you're using currently. Is it working successfully for you? How could it be better?

Is there room for growth and expansion within the software? Do you think it will last for the next three to five years? Do several different brands of software within your organization accomplish the same task? Does the software manufacturer make regular enhancements to it, and do you have the most current version? Can you move data from one application to another if necessary? Is there a network version of the software available? If so, what are the advantages of using it versus stand-alone? Is the software you're using an industry-standard package known to almost everyone, or an obscure package that only a handful of people use?

Using Standardized Software

In many organizations, software is a personal choice—these *are* personal computers, right? Yes, up to a point. Unless information is shared physically among users, there's little need for standardized software packages. Word processing seems to be the area where the largest variety of packages appear. I have worked for companies that had 20 different word processing packages. Some people were using different packages for different word processing tasks—running the gamut from a simple, public domain text editor to complicated desktop publishing packages.

However, with a networked environment, many benefits can be derived from software standards. When word processing or spreadsheet files are transferred among various people on the network, no translation is required, and loss of special formatting is unlikely. Individual computers become more standardized, allowing people to physically shift to another machine with ease. Training can be coordinated for several individuals at one time, and special productivity techniques can be developed to allow for easier use of the product. If you do not have standards for software among your personal computers, you may want to re-evaluate when you go to a network.

What Is Standard Applications Software?

Standard applications software is software that has been accepted by the market to be highly efficient and user-friendly for specific tasks, relatively free of software "bugs," and supported over an extended period of time by the developers of the program.

Perhaps the model has been set by Lotus, with its 1-2-3 application. Millions of users have purchased a computer solely for the power and flexibility that Lotus offers, and an entire follow-on market has developed around this standard. Despite stiff competition and some false starts with program changes, Lotus 1-2-3 is likely to remain the standard spreadsheet software.

The same situation exists for word processing, where WordPerfect has emerged at the top of the heap, with its market share growing every year.

Why Go with the Standards?

Using standard applications software has a number of advantages over lesser-known packages, especially for those who are less technically inclined:

Well-Traveled Road: Because a large number of these applications are in use, chances are good that they're already tested and mostly error-free for your particular needs.

Follow-on Products: For major applications software, entire follow-on markets have developed, providing additional software tools such as books, video tapes and other supplementary items. For example, with R&R Report Writer from Concentric Technologies, the average dBASE user can easily produce complicated reports that are beyond the inherent capabilities of dBASE alone.

Most standard software companies publish catalogs listing products offered by independent developers to enhance their software. WordPerfect's catalog, for example, features dictionaries, spell-checkers, graphics tools, macro libraries and other aids.

Training: Because of the exposure of these standard software products, there's a large body of experience to draw upon when help is needed. For any standard software, many beginning or advanced books are available, and training can usually be obtained within an hour's drive of almost anywhere. Schools for the most part use standard packages in their classroom training; consultants typically support and are most familiar with the standard applications.

Ease of Acquiring Personnel: When making hiring decisions, previous experience with appropriate software often is a big plus, and a necessity in some cases. Imagine the training curve you're in for if a new administrative assistant knows Wang word processing and your company uses WordPerfect exclusively. Such temporary agencies as Kelly Services and Manpower now test applicants to ensure a certain level of expertise in spreadsheet and word processing programs before sending them out on assignments. Needless to say, they test only on standard software packages.

Hardware Manufacturer Support: For hardware-intensive applications, or those that require special hardware components for maximum use, hardware manufacturers cater to the standards first. For example, new, specialized video monitors will almost invariably include a device driver for AutoCAD, instantly creating a market of more than 180,000 potential customers. Those same manufacturers are less likely to support a lesser-known applications package.

User Groups: In almost any city here or abroad, Lotus 1-2-3 or dBASE III user groups meet periodically to discuss better use of the software. New users can realize tremendous benefits in terms of problem-solving and staying up-to-date on new trends, applications, etc.

Integration: Nearly any software product can communicate with dBASE, Lotus and several word processors. The standard data files from these applications have rapidly become industry standards, allowing movement of data among programs. Only a few years ago, this was impossible (or the exclusive territory of the "guru" who understood assembly language programming and hex dumps of the computer's internal memory). For example, data can be taken out of dBASE, passed to Lotus 1-2-3 and copied into the annual report being created with Microsoft Word.

Technical Support: Each industry-standard software package has a large support network in place to handle functional and technical questions, as well as bulletins and newsletters. Many dealers offer free support or support contracts for these packages, or you can usually purchase support contracts from companies that specialize exclusively in supporting these products. Only the standards have a large enough user base to warrant widespread support.

Future Potential: New and innovative software packages are always being introduced, and it will be interesting to look at the standards of a decade hence to see if Lotus 1-2-3 will still be at the top of the list, or if some other application will relegate Lotus to the "retired hero" position that the original VisiCalc occupies today. The software world is becoming increasingly dominated by the large software companies that have the financial and technical resources to support a large number of end users and the increasing complexity of personal computing. Microsoft, Lotus, Ashton-Tate, WordPerfect and Autodesk were the top five personal computer software companies in 1987, with combined revenues of more than $1.5 billion dollars and users numbering in the tens of millions. This revenue allows these companies to pour money back into research and development and to continue improving existing products.

If the above list seems to make a strong case for using standard applications software, this is in fact a good strategy when an organization needs consistent results without devoting a lot of time to researching software options. This isn't to say that alternative software packages on the market don't sometimes offer superior performance at less cost. However, when you have other headaches to deal with, staying conservative with software may be the best route.

In some cases, there may be a certain application you need in your organization that isn't found in standard software. One that comes to mind is the ability to store a graphics (picture) file within a database record. As this book goes to press, no market-leading database packages offer that capability. If you were a realtor who had determined that the single critical success factor of a "homes listing" database was a visual representation of the home, you would be forced to use software that wasn't a market standard.

What About Software Clones?

Most standard applications packages have "clone" versions available. Produced by other companies, clones are designed to look and feel like the leading software but cost much less. For example, VP Planner is an almost exact duplication of Lotus 1-2-3 as far as features and capabilities go. It can read Lotus files directly, and virtually all the commands are the same. Yet VP Planner is considerably less expensive than Lotus 1-2-3.

In some cases, the clone software outperforms the standards as well as providing additional features. FoxBASE+ from Fox Software runs database programs from two to five times faster than the market-leading dBASE III Plus, in addition to providing several invaluable functions not yet available from Ashton-Tate.

To Clone or Not to Clone

The decision to use a software clone within your business should not be taken lightly, and should be tied closely to your mission-critical systems. If a function is critical to your business, I would recommend paying the extra money for the proven software product to make that function a success. For less vital functions, give the clone software a try, particularly if the clone has been around awhile and enjoys near-standard status itself (much like Compaq in the hardware arena).

You can also have a mixture of software if you don't mind a little administrative work. Give the standard package to those people who do a lot of critical spreadsheet work, and give clone software to those casual users who don't go far beyond the simple row-and-column addition of numbers or who review the work of others. Using a look-alike package that can easily accept and transport files that the leading software can read can save a substantial amount of money.

Administrative work associated with look-alike packages involves slightly different procedures and installation methods, and multiple upgrades may be required. Political issues are also involved; for instance, someone may feel slighted because he or she is using the cheaper package.

Network Versions

Many vendors of leading PC software offer network versions as well. Typically, the software is installed on the central file server and allows a specified number of users to run the software from their local PCs. The software is copied from the file server's hard disk into the main memory of the local PC for execution. Data may be stored on the file server or the local PC.

The network version of software may contain additional features that allow printer access and many people to share a single data file on the network server. This is especially important in database applications, where many users may need to share centralized information for their own particular tasks.

If you have a software package that's important to your business, check to see how it works with each networking solution you're considering. If compatibility isn't possible with a particular network solution, you may need to eliminate that option.

File- and Record-Locking: An important note should be made about network access to information. Information can be accessed in two major ways—file-locking and record-locking. File-locking is a technique that denies access to data when another person is using it. One user and one user only can access a spreadsheet or word processing document file. If several people were working simultaneously on the same spreadsheet file, someone could be changing numbers behind you without your knowledge.

Record-locking is used primarily in database applications; it allows a number of people to access the same file of information concurrently. For example, several people in a company may access the customer master file: sales can place an order and check credit, accounts receivable can apply cash received, and shipping can print shipping documents. Conflicts occur when different users want the same record. Most database software is designed to handle this gracefully, making one process wait until the other is completed.

Picking Your Network DBMS: A Critical Issue

For most organizations, *the* critical piece of network software is the network database management system (DBMS). The database software you choose will be used by a number of people across the organization, and it should be chosen carefully. Here are some items to consider in this evaluation:

Functionality: Does the database perform all tasks necessary to support everyone on the network? Forms? Reports? Ad hoc inquiry?

Ease of Use and Power Trade-offs: Can the database be used by novices with minimal training, yet still provide the trained user with a rich environment for development of complex applications?

Compatibility/Scalability: Can the database be moved to another machine or operating system in the event you outgrow your current hardware? For example, Informix's database product can run on a PC, many Unix machines, a VAX or several other machines. dBASE IV runs only under MS-DOS and OS/2. If you expect a high level of growth, picking a single database that can handle the needs of your organization will save time and money later.

Applications Packages: Are there applications packages that have been developed with the database that will allow your company to avoid the expense and time involved with custom software? For example, you might want to use the same database for your accounting system and your mailing labels. This approach allows greater flexibility in dealing with your data.

Security Features: How is access to data controlled? Can sensitive data be protected from individuals who should not be able to read or change it?

Future: What does the vendor have planned for future developments, and how does the vendor's strategy affect your plans for using the product?

Support: Does the vendor offer technical support locally? Are instruction books and other learning aids available?

Supplementary Products: Are there products that work in conjunction with the database to provide even greater access or development tools? For example, R&R Report Writer is an excellent report writer for dBASE III that allows easy access to many database files.

Memory/System Requirements: Will the product work well in the environment you're planning? For example, some products are designed to work with small databases on older PCs, while others demand extended or expanded memory to function at all.

Data Import/Export Facilities: Can the package easily read in data from other sources within your organization (e.g., spreadsheets, other databases, etc.)? What formats does the package support for taking data out of the database for transfer to other packages?

Price: Price is important, but there are other things to consider. Does the package allow an unlimited number of users for a network version, or is it necessary to buy additional licenses for each group of five users?

The Client/Server Model for Databases

A revolution is beginning to take place within the networked database world. In MS-DOS-based networks, database software runs on the local workstations and can access only server databases in total. All processing is done after copying records across the network to the local workstation. This approach can create heavy network traffic and slow down long inquiries.

With advanced networks under OS/2, the server can provide advanced database services for the workstation. When the workstation issues a request for information, the server can process this request, passing back only the "answer" to the workstation. This eliminates a lot of network traffic and enables advanced database applications not previously possible or feasible.

For example, say you had a dBASE III Plus application running on a 3Com network. Your database file has 10,000 records, and you want to search for any database record with the character string "1.1" embedded in the description field. When this query is run, each of the records is copied across the network into the memory of the local workstation, where it's examined and, in most cases, discarded.

In the client/server database, the same request would be passed to the server: find all of the records with "1.1" somewhere in the description field. The difference would be in the processing: the server would look through the records in the database, identify the ones matching the criterion, and pass them back to the workstation (maybe 50 records, rather than 10,000). This reduces network traffic and speeds up the search process significantly. If the workstation was running OS/2 or Unix, it could be performing other tasks while waiting for the database request to finish.

Ashton-Tate, Microsoft and Sybase have teamed up to develop and market the SQL server, an advanced database server running on OS/2. One of the advantages of this product is that it allows a multitude of front-end processes to access the database, giving spreadsheets and other programs similar access to a database.

Multi-User Software

The software we've discussed up to this point has been single-user software (i.e., an application such as word processing, where one individual operates the computer to produce one specific output at a time). At that point, the paper output or computer data file can be passed on to someone else for review or some other process, but only one person is working with the live data at one time.

Multi-user software is much more dynamic; it comes into play when a network among several computers is set up. Information is then shared among several individuals, allowing one single copy of information to serve the needs of many.

A good example of a multi-user application can be found in SBT's Accounting Library, a series of software modules written in dBASE III. When this software is run across a computer network like 3Com or Novell, the data files are located on the central file server(s) and are shared among the various users. The receiving dock can be entering receipts against open purchase orders while the purchasing department is creating new purchase orders and accounts payable can be printing checks for vendors owed for previous deliveries.

The Vendor Master File is used by all three of these different applications to provide specific information about vendors and to update with new information: the receiving dock lowers the vendors' total in the on-order amount field at the same time the purchasing department might be buying more and raising the on-order amount. Accounts payable, by cutting a check for the amount owed the vendor, lowers the total outstanding balance of the vendor and updates total yearly purchases.

Multi-user software can come in several flavors—open, closed or somewhere in between. A totally open system would come with the source code included and use a standard industry database format. A totally closed system would have no source code and use a proprietary method of storing data within the application.

Each company should assess which type of package it needs during the evaluation phase. It can be very frustrating to find out that the package cannot be changed if that was a high priority that was ignored. Many companies feel better if the software cannot be changed, especially in the financial accounting area. These are important issues that should be carefully considered by both management and technical departments of the organization.

Electronic Mail

Another multi-user-oriented application is electronic mail (E-mail). An electronic mail system set up on a network allows all connected computer users to send and receive messages from others on the computer network. It also accommodates any remote users who have access to the network's mail system, either through remote log-ins (using a modem and PC), or through a gateway to one of the commercial E-mail systems like MCI Mail.

In many organizations with more than ten individuals, this application alone can justify a network. Interruptions are minimized, meetings avoided, and more people can provide feedback on a particular issue; an electronic record of messages can be kept for a particular subject if desired.

Organizations that are widely dispersed can benefit from consolidating noncritical messages and sending them during the hours when phone rates are lower, avoiding costly prime-time conversations. E-mail can lower costs and enhance communication; it's particularly valuable in instances where there are time differences or when someone is out of town or cannot be interrupted to take a phone call.

The use of E-mail is spreading rapidly, with more and more businesses realizing its benefits. In one company where I installed E-mail, meetings dropped by 30 percent, and communications were improved tremendously. After the initial installation for people who already had personal computers, those who formerly wouldn't have used a computer were demanding access to the network.

By logically grouping people who use E-mail, addressing a large audience with a question or proposal is easy. For example, there might be a group called Sales (which would include Bill, Sally and Jean). By sending a memo via E-mail to the group, people could address the entire group simultaneously and avoid typing extra names. People also can be easily added or deleted from the group.

With remote access to an E-mail system, people who are traveling can routinely check their mail using a lap-top computer or a computer they borrow along the way. While dialing into a LAN isn't as easy or effective as using a dial-in terminal on a microcomputer, exchanging E-mail or other simple tasks can be accomplished.

Work Group Software

As LANs become more and more popular, new software packages are becoming available that exploit the full potential of networked computers. One package designed specifically for a network application is For Comment from Broderbund Software. This package allows a work group to review word-processed material, make comments and edits, and distribute the material for review by many individuals within the organization.

What was previously accomplished by a paper routing sheet and a hard copy of the document can now be handled electronically. Revisions, if desired, can be automatically incorporated into the document without retyping, and each person can see the revisions suggested by others.

Another example of work group software is the Coordinator (Action Technologies). This innovative package, when supported by management, can become the hub for calendars, action items and other communications between many individuals. Commitments can be made and tracked as well.

Many additional software packages are being developed for use within work groups. Software development, drawing management and document processing are areas being developed beyond the individual user and into the cooperative processing arena.

Deciding Factors

The decisions you make in selecting applications software can mean success or failure as you move toward sharing information within your organization. The right software will make your strategy soar, providing benefits and reaffirming your decision. The wrong applications software can slow you down and cause frustration with the entire project. No amount of premium hardware will make up for inadequate software.

New applications that are emerging will be more network-dependent, addressing the need for enhanced communications between work groups and people. E-mail will continue to grow rapidly, expanding into a universal approach toward exchanging information.

Consider the following factors when you're deciding on software.

1. The software you choose will have a major effect on the success of your system.

2. Industry-standard software is a good choice when you don't want to take chances.

3. Clone software can offer substantial savings when used properly.

4. Follow-on products offered for best-selling software should be investigated. They usually solve any weaknesses within the software.

5. Keep everything as standard as possible; supporting a multitude of different products for the same task is frustrating, time-consuming, and rarely worth the effort.

6. Network (multi-user) versions of software can save money and minimize exposure to illegal software copying.

7. Electronic mail is one of the major groupware products for enhancing productivity. Watch for new developments in this area.

Moving On

We've looked at the planning, short-term alternatives and software so far. In the next chapters, we'll look at all the components that make up a full-fledged LAN. If it gets confusing, refer back to your goals—that should help you sort through what's most important and what's not worth the confusion. In many cases, you can take the "default" option and you'll do just fine. The key is to know which areas are particularly important to your business.

7

Network Topologies

In this chapter, we'll examine network setups available to your organization and the trade-offs among the various configurations.

In order to preserve simplicity and avoid technical overload, we'll start at the summary level. Once you know the basics (which aren't likely to change in the near future), additional information can be obtained from books and magazines that can provide up-to-the-minute technical information in regard to this rapidly changing environment.

The goal of this chapter in particular—and the book in general—is to demystify some of the technical verbiage thrown around whenever networking decisions are discussed by people "in the know." Often, this is simply "techno-babble" that's irrelevant or secondary to the overall task you want to accomplish.

The Evolution of Topologies

Networks were first developed for mainframes and minicomputers. At that point they were fairly simple: one type of network software ran on one type of cabling, and computers had to be the same type—take it or leave it. If you bought DEC gear, you had to connect to DEC equipment to make it work.

Now the rigidity is relaxing. For example, when I first saw EtherNet used, it was a large, mysterious, expensive, yellow cable that few people understood. EtherNet today can be run over thick, durable cable; thin, lightweight 50 OHM coax (thin EtherNet); unshielded phone wire (twisted pairs); fiber optic cable; or any combination of the above that conforms to the EtherNet IEEE 802.3 specification.

Although this flexibility is beneficial to the end user, it also makes the initial choices more complex.

Always keep in mind that the best network configuration for your organization is one that will meet the needs of your business both now and in the future. Certainly, look at the specifications provided by the vendors who quote on your network, but also go out and look at some networks in action in companies similar to your own.

As discussed in previous chapters, it's best to identify the best solution for your needs before you get into budgeting; otherwise, you may move toward low-cost solutions without giving the others a chance. Token Ring and EtherNet, for example, can cost more or less per network node solution, depending largely on the cable and the network cards you use. If you decide exclusively on price, you might fulfill your short-term needs but paint yourself into a corner in terms of future expansion.

With these suggestions in mind, let's explore some of the options.

Networks can be configured in a variety of ways, but the three basic methods are bus, ring and star. Many permutations can be drawn from these basic methods (active star, token bus, dual ring, etc.).

Bus Network

A bus network looks simpler than either the ring or the star. The network is a single piece of cable terminated on each end. Each of the nodes is attached to the central network cable with a transceiver cable that connects to the PC.

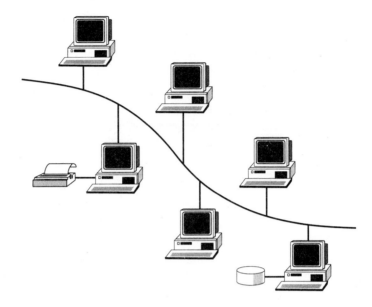

Figure 7.1   Bus network: a linear configuration.

Bus networks use a technique called *broadcasting*. When a network node transmits information, it's sent to all nodes at the same time. Each node checks to see if the information is addressed to it. If the receiving node ascertains that the information was received correctly, an acknowledgment is sent to the sending workstation. EtherNet is the most widely implemented bus-type network.

Because all nodes receive the transmissions concurrently, broadcast networks have a greater performance range than star or ring networks. If one of the nodes is disabled, this will not affect the remainder of the nodes. Disruption or damage to the main network cable can be devastating, causing all nodes to be out of commission until remedied.

Ring Network

In a ring network, all the computers are literally connected with a continuous ring of cable. When data are passed around the ring from one node to another, each node in turn analyzes the data being sent, and if it isn't addressed to the examining node, the information is passed to the next node, etc., until assimilated by the proper station. IBM's Token Ring is the most popular ring network.

Ring networks require much less cable than star networks, and they don't require a central processor. If, however, the network is broken at any point, all network stations can be affected. This vulnerability can be compensated for in a number of ways, each requiring redundant cables.

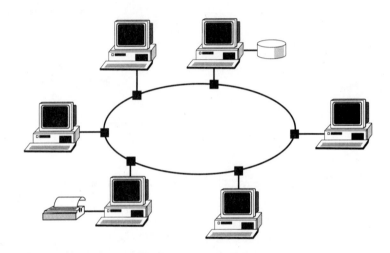

Figure 7.2   Ring network: what goes around comes around.

Star Network

The star network was the original network configuration, and it is still used extensively today. Telephone switches operate on a star concept, as do many host-based networks (e.g., a minicomputer with a series of individually connected dumb terminals).

The star network has a device or hub that acts as the traffic cop for all network requests. Each device must have a direct path to the hub, and if the central hub is not operational, the entire network is down as well. However, losing one of the nodes on the network doesn't affect the rest of the network. AT&T's StarLan is an example of this type of network.

The star configuration has been showing up in many networks that previously used either the bus or ring configuration. This is due to the fault tolerance built into the star (i.e., one node going off-line doesn't affect the entire network or segment). Both EtherNet and Token Ring networks can run in a star-type configuration, which is particularly popular in implementations using twisted-pair wiring. Having many distributed hubs can help minimize the impact of any broken portion of the network.

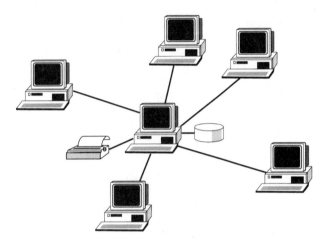

Figure 7.3   Star network: a hub operation.

Proceed with Care

Some books and articles about network configuration choices use sweeping categorizations. For example, it's often stated that Token Ring's networks are consistently slow, or that EtherNet is always one large bus-type network and as such is unreliable and prone to over-loading. In fact, EtherNet can be configured in a variety of ways to fit the needs of your organization, giving reliable, low-cost, high-quality performance. Token Ring's performance will be perfectly acceptable for the majority of applications and is being implemented in many major networks. It's preferred where consistent perfor-mance is necessary (e.g., the shop floor).

If any of the networks were as poor as they're reported to be in some of the literature, they wouldn't have enjoyed such widespread success in the past.

Ask a lot of questions of your network vendor. If you feel confused or that the advice you've received is biased, get another opinion. If your vendor doesn't install a particular type of network, the salesperson should take responsibility for finding someone else who knows about its pros and cons.

Major Network Access Methods

Communicating between devices on the network is similar to people talking—there must be a common means for sending and receiving messages, and those messages must be understandable to both parties exchanging information. Let's look at the most common methods utilized today.

EtherNet

This is the most popular network; it's used in a wide variety of networks, both large and small. EtherNet was developed by Bob Metcalfe, who worked for Xerox during the early Seventies and later founded 3Com, one of the major network software companies. EtherNet is a broadcast network: when a device wants to use the network, it listens to see if someone else is using the network and then broadcasts its message. If another station transmits at the same time, a collision occurs and each workstation waits a random amount of time before retrying.

A nontechnical example of this technique might be a room full of people having a discussion without any particular rules of order. Each person must wait for an opening to speak, and if two people accidentally speak at the same time, both people must stop, wait a random amount of time, and then try again.

As the number of stations grows, there's increased contention for the use of the cable, resulting in degraded performance. Usually this happens only in networks exceeding 100 nodes; it can be compensated for by using smaller "subnets" that can limit the amount of traffic processed on each network. Following are the pros and cons of an EtherNet network.

Pros

High Speed: EtherNet has a rated band width of ten megabits per second, making it one of the fastest network solutions available.

Multimedia: As mentioned previously, EtherNet can be run over several media types: thick coax, thin coax, broad-band cable, telephone wiring (shielded and unshielded) and fiber-optic cable, as well as a mixture of cabling schemes.

Extensibility: While EtherNet can become overloaded with collisions if used heavily by many devices, it can also be segmented into small, logical networks to reduce traffic without limiting access to all nodes on the network. Devices called *bridges* can be used to filter traffic between networks, reducing contention for the cable and the impact of a cable break.

Multiple Protocols: Many types of network software can be run over the same cable, allowing great flexibility and future expansion. For example, multiple PCs and PC file servers (running 3Com's 3+ network software) might share the same cable with several Sun Microsystems machines running Unix and some Macintoshes running the TOPS network. This avoids having to run multiple types of cables within a facility that has many types of machines. This fact alone has made EtherNet the *de facto* standard for large organizations that network many types of computers.

Universal Acceptance: EtherNet supports by far the largest number of devices that can be attached directly to it. EtherNet connections are offered as standard equipment on many workstations; for example, the standard for all Sun workstations and larger DEC VAX computers includes an EtherNet port.

Cons

Contention: Due to the broadcast method by which devices access the network, collisions can occur on the network and degrade performance.

Cost per Node: Because of EtherNet's many capabilities and high speed, the cabling and network cards necessary to run the network tend to be more expensive than some of the simpler solutions.

Security: Because all information is broadcast to all the devices on the network, security could be a problem if a malicious and talented "hacker" gained access to the network.

Token Ring

Token Ring networks are becoming popular, ranking second behind EtherNet in installed networks. Token Ring networks use a mechanism called *token passing* to determine network access by the devices on the network. An electronic token is passed from workstation to workstation; and a device can access the network only when it possesses the token.

Again, using our nontechnical examples, token passing is somewhat like passing around a microphone at a conference table. Each person is given a turn at the microphone. If he or she has nothing to say, the microphone is passed to the next person, and so on. While this gives consistent performance, large, lightly loaded networks can experience a delay as the token is passed around the network looking for work. When someone decides to send a message, it isn't broadcast to the entire network, but only to the addressed station.

Token Ring has been gaining popularity in areas where response time is consistent and predictable. Shop-floor data collection is an example of an application that benefits from predictable network response.

Token Ring networks come in two speeds: 4MB per second and 16MB per second (recently released). The latter is more expensive, and you should weigh the needs of your business when deciding between the two speeds.

Pros

Deterministic Performance: Because each workstation gets the opportunity to transmit in sequence, performance will degrade very slowly as additional nodes are added to the network.

IBM Sanction: Token Ring is IBM's sanctioned networking scheme, and this has an impact on companies that have a lot of IBM mainframe or midrange computer equipment. For the foreseeable future, IBM will also be around to support and enhance Token Ring.

Fault Tolerance: By using additional cable and setting up multiple routes for the token, the impact of the cable break can be minimized.

Cons

Limited Usage: At this writing, many types of computers don't have Token Ring support, including DEC and many Unix-based systems. If your organization needs the capability to connect disparate items of equipment together, this limitation can create problems.

problems. However, expect this problem to become less critical as Token Ring becomes more universal.

Cost: Token Ring is among the most expensive network topologies.

Additional Cable Expense: This will be required to ensure fault tolerance and redundancy for all nodes on the network.

ARCNET

Developed by Datapoint in the 1970s, ARCNET is one of the original network access methods. It's a very popular method that uses a token-passing method on a multistar topology.

Pros

Cost: ARCNET cards are among the least expensive for fully functional networks.

Flexibility: ARCNET can be run on a number of cabling schemes.

Trouble-shooting: The multiple hubs allow easier location of faulty nodes or cable.

Cons

Speed: ARCNET is the slowest of the three leading networks. This can be perfectly adequate for many networks, however, and shouldn't be an eliminating factor in itself.

Future: As sales of Token Ring and EtherNet increase and as faster network methods materialize on the horizon, enhancements to ARCNET are unclear.

As of this writing, ARCNET doesn't support 32-bit workstations, so if you're looking at 32-bit workstations, you need to explore other configurations.

Network Cabling Schemes

The network cabling choice you make is very important to the success of your entire network; it comprises a significant portion of the hardware cost you're likely to incur. If you equate a network to a city, the cabling would be the equivalent of the roads, and the workstations and servers the houses or buildings. Deciding the type road for your network is very important from a cost and reliability standpoint.

Choosing and installing the proper type of network media can result in years of trouble-free operation. The wrong type of media can cause frequent breakdowns and network failures and be a source of frustration with the overall operation of the LAN you choose.

Coaxial Cable

Durable, easily spliced, and relatively inexpensive, *Coax* is the traditional network medium. It comes in a variety of sizes for different types of networks. It's composed of a metal core (either solid or braided) surrounded by insulation and grounding material.

For EtherNet networks, two types of coax cable, *thick* and *thin*, are typically used.

Thick, or *standard*, EtherNet is heavy-duty, thick cable which is used for the backbone segments of the network. To connect a device to thick EtherNet cable, a special *vampire* tap is used along with a transceiver cable.

Thin EtherNet is used in conjunction with BNC connectors. BNC connectors are easily crimped or spliced onto connectors that join pieces of thin coax cable together and provide the interface to the networking card. Thin EtherNet is much more flexible and less expensive than thick EtherNet; however, it's not as durable. This type of coax wiring is suffering strong competition from twisted pair, which may eventually overtake it in popularity.

Twisted Pair

Twisted-pair network cabling can be installed using ordinary telephone wiring. This type of networking is a fairly recent innovation for high-speed systems. Its reliability can be enhanced by using shielded wire, but this usually necessitates running new wire rather than using the existing wiring in the building—one of the primary reasons that twisted pair is desirable. EtherNet's popularity over twisted-pair wiring has exploded during 1989. This is because the cost of twisted-pair equipment has been dropping and its reliability has improved greatly. Twisted pair lowers the number of stations on a segment (most often to one station). Thus, if a segment is broken, fewer workstations are affected by the break.

Fiber Optics

Fiber-optic cable is one of the newest media used for networks; it seems to offer great potential for the future. The cable is composed of slender glass threads surrounded by insulating and cushioning material that carry network signals at very high speeds. Most advanced networks use fiber optics as the main cable. Recent advances with plastic fiber optics promise a new generation of rugged and inexpensive fiber-optic cable.

FDDI

Fiber Distributed Data Interface (FDDI) is a new standard being developed in conjunction with fiber-optic cable. It offers the highest commercially available network capacity/band width: 100MB per second. FDDI is based on a dual-path, counter-rotating Token Ring topology. Currently, prices for FDDI connections are very expensive but should fall within the range of average users over the next several years.

Developers today are working on fiber-based networks that can handle gigabyte-per-second throughput. This is the equivalent of transmitting almost 3,000 360K floppy disks full of information in one second! While this type of throughput isn't currently necessary, except in extreme circumstances, future developments in workstations and user interfaces may make even these band widths seem slow and inadequate.

When to Use What

Picking the type of cable to use can be difficult. Use the following guidelines and talk to your vendors about what they recommend and can demonstrate at reference sites.

Use thick EtherNet when . . .

- it's a rugged environment (very durable).
- long distances must be covered.
- moves and changes are infrequent.

Use thin EtherNet when . . .

- expenses must be kept down.
- changes and moves are very frequent.
- twisted pair's not available.

Use twisted pair when . . .

- extra reliable phone wire already exists.
- minimal disruption to the network is desired.
- add-ons, moves and changes are frequent.
- aesthetics are important (least noticeable).

Use fiber optics when . . .

- you have point-to-point backbone connections.
- future high-band-width networks will be needed.
- security is key (fiber can't be tapped easily).

Specialty Methods

For special circumstances, there are many specialized ways to extend a network. Traditional *leased telephone lines* can be used to connect far-flung buildings. *Microwave* and *infrared* devices can be used to connect buildings that have a direct line-of-site path at very high speeds. *Satellite networks* can also be used to connect geographically separated networks at high speeds. Each of these access methods has its pros and cons that should be examined in detail before proceeding with an installation.

Mixing and Matching

In most environments, the types of media discussed in this chapter can be mixed and matched to provide a wide range of options for configuration. Your company should take into account current and future needs when determining the cable access method. If business expansion involves moving into new buildings, running fiber to each office could pay large, long-term dividends. In addition to traditional data applications, future networks must be able to send voice, data and video transmissions to the workstations.

If such expense cannot be justified, you should at least plan for cable upgrades. Rewiring older buildings could cause the organization to suffer expense and delay when installing 1990s technology into an 1890s building.

Moving On

If you managed to understand most of this chapter, you're in a good position to think about and analyze the type of network method and cable scheme that is most appropriate for your organization. In Chapter 8, we'll look at the components that plug into the network—servers, workstations, etc. You'll get a complete picture of the pieces your organization would need if a network were set up.

Remember your business goals for the network. It's here in the technical portion that goals tend to slip away and the project becomes a technical free-for-all. Keep looking at what you're trying to accomplish in terms of benefitting the organization.

8

Network Components

Now that you're familiar with basic network topologies and cabling options, let's look at the components that make up a typical PC network. On a small network, things are pretty simple, requiring only the PCs, the central file server, the method for connecting the computers, the network cards that go into the workstations and file servers (see attached diagram) and the software that makes them all "talk." As you add more stations and capabilities or mix multiple network types together, things can get more complex, but the basic operation is the same.

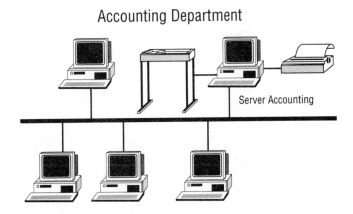

Figure 8.1   Making connections: the components of a basic network.

Hardware

File Servers

The file server is the device you designate as the central resource for the network. In a small network, there may be only one file server; in a large network, there may be many. Choosing the correct file server is important and there are several things to consider.

Proprietary or Standard?

Several hardware manufacturers offer proprietary servers specially designed to be network file servers. These devices—such as 3Com's 3S/400—might offer 386 processors, high-speed/large-capacity disk drive(s), high-capacity backup devices, and room for additional expansion options. These servers are designed to be very reliable, running 24 hours a day for many months without failure.

On the negative side, these servers cannot be used as stand-alone workstations in the event of a network problem. When repairs are needed, they must be made by an authorized dealer. If the dedicated server becomes obsolete, it cannot be easily absorbed into the organization.

Using a standard workstation (such as an IBM AT or Compaq 386) as a server can have several advantages. First, since the device is a normal PC, it can be used as such if the network breaks. In addition to that advantage, it's usually easier to get reliable repair service on standard computers, and to obtain upgrades in terms of disks, memory and other devices.

Many of the new computers offer a fast processor and can be configured with high-speed drives and an expanded amount of memory. At this writing, many computer manufacturers offer 25MHZ performance. Some vendors also offer mirrored disk drives, a feature previously found only on dedicated servers. If the workstation being used as a server becomes outmoded, it can easily be moved into service as a workstation.

A note about clones: I have seen companies use cheap clone computers as their network servers. Some worked fine and others caused big problems in terms of compatibility and reliability. If you're going to buy any name-brand equipment, the server is the item to spend the extra money on.

Capabilities

Before investing in a file server, first analyze what it will be doing. In a network that's used a lot for interactive data-sharing (e.g, many people accessing accounting and inventory information concurrently), you need a fast processor, expanded memory and a fast disk drive (or drives). However, if your file server is used only occasionally, for such tasks as individual file transfer, print spooling or for storing electronic mail, you might not need a high-capacity server.

Performance

Consider the following when assessing file-server performance:

Processor Speed: 80286 and 80386 machines come in several speeds; for example, the 80386 can be purchased with speeds of 16MHZ, 20MHZ, 25MHZ and 33MHZ clock speeds. The greater the clock speed, the faster your CPU performance.

Disk Speed: Disk speeds are important; the fastest CPU will not overcome a sluggish hard disk. Items to check are the *access speed* (under 30 milliseconds is good; under 20 is preferred for applications doing large amounts of disk work such as database searches). *Interleave factor* is another consideration. The interleave factor relates to the length of time it takes to read a cylinder of data on the hard disk. If the interleave factor is 3, the disk must go through three complete spins before reading all the data. If the disk is fast enough, and the interleave factor is 1, it must wait only one revolution to read the data. Obviously, an interleave factor of 1 is better than 2 or 3. In most DOS-based networks, the size, speed and number of disks will be a major factor in the performance of the network.

Hardware/Software Caching: Depending on how they're implemented, caching (storing the most frequently used data in a memory buffer), can help speed access tremendously. Hardware caching is preferable since it doesn't detract from your available memory (RAM). Many CPU vendors include hardware caching on their advanced offerings.

Memory (RAM): This is very important; with advanced networks, you can hardly have too much RAM. Your vendor should be able to analyze how much memory you will need for your workload. If possible, buy even more than he or she recommends—you'll be amazed at how soon you'll need it.

Printer Ports: Check the number of printer ports that are standard equipment on the file server against what you'll need. Ensure that additional ports can be added to accommodate at least your next two years worth of printing needs. Some PCs are limited in the number of serial or parallel ports they can support; purchasing an expensive network and then having to use an AB switch to access printers could be frustrating!

Host-Based Servers

Third-party software is available for several leading networks that enables them to use an existing minicomputer, such as a VAX or Sun Microsystems Unix mini, as a LAN file server. This capability can offer a variety of benefits, including scheduled backups, access to corporate databases and better utilization of existing resources. In most of the recent implementations, data can be stored and retrieved without conversion.

Dedicated or Nondedicated Servers

Several of the leading networks allow PCs to perform double duty as both a server and a workstation. With an MS-DOS-based network, this arrangement is awkward and leaves little memory for the user of the workstation acting as a server.

However, with advanced OS/2 networks that break the memory barriers established under MS-DOS, this will become a more common practice. An administrative person could perform word processing on a machine also serving the entire network with customer information.

Use caution with this scenario. A person using the server as a workstation might inadvertently shut off the machine while network processing is occurring—not a good thing to do! Also, sensitive network data could be accidentally (or deliberately) destroyed or modified.

Network Interface Card

The network interface card is the connection between the computer and the network media (the cable, wire or whatever you use). These cards come in a wide variety of choices, with several types available for each kind of network. For example, 3Com makes a variety of cards that allow IBM PCs and compatibles to be attached to either thick or thin EtherNet cable. These cards are installed inside the expansion bus on the PC, with the cable connector protruding from the back of the machine.

When deciding which type of card to use, consider the following:

Reliability: Make sure that the cards you buy were made by a reputable, reliable manufacturer. The last thing you need is problems with your network cards. Cards can be very hard to debug.

Cost: The cost is important since you'll need one card for every machine you put on the network. For simplicity's sake, avoid mixing many brands.

Speed: Most cards are rated by how fast they can transfer data from the PC to the network. Check the numbers, but keep in mind that they may not affect your application heavily unless you frequently do large data transfers.

Compatibility: Some cards do not have the necessary drivers included to work on certain networks, and this can be very troublesome. If you use an outside vendor and this problem occurs, it's likely that you're being experimented with.

Intelligent/Nonintelligent: Some cards come with on-board memory that allows faster transfer and, more importantly, the capability for loading some of the network software on the card rather than taking up precious DOS RAM.

The EtherLink+ card offered by 3Com has 256K of memory installed on the card. This accommodates most of the network drivers, eliminating much of the overhead associated with installing the software in the limited 640K that MS-DOS offers. The card also offers faster throughput of information by using the memory on the card as a storage buffer. These cards are known as intelligent adapters, and cost more than standard cards. If you can afford them, they'll give more capability and have a longer useful life.

Network Media (coax, twisted pair, fiber)

This is the actual cable or wiring (described in Chapter 7) that connects the individual workstations and the file servers together. Deciding which media to use for your network may seem like a small item, but it is very important and can have a large impact on the cost of a network.

Utilizing existing twisted-pair wiring is often a good option, but care should be taken to test all wires that will be used before the actual installation. In an EtherNet environment, many companies use a "backbone" network of either thick coaxial cable or fiber optic cable. From that backbone, other media can be used to connect individual segments. The options are very flexible: twisted pair could be used for an executive office area where appearances are important, while a cubicle area could be wired with thin, flexible EtherNet cable.

Workstations

The workstations in a LAN environment can be the same PCs used before the LAN was installed, but the existence of the LAN opens up other possibilities as well.

Diskless Workstations are offered by many of the leading computer vendors. These devices download the software needed to run from the network server when they're turned on or rebooted. The advantages of these devices are simplicity, economy and security. One of the problems associated with diskless nodes is their total dependence on the network file server. If the file server becomes disabled, the workstation is useless.

Portable Computers coupled with a network adapter can serve double duty as portable computer and full-fledged network node. This arrangement allows individuals who travel frequently to avoid the expense of duplicate equipment for office and travel. Only portables that have an expansion slot built in or those that allow an external expansion slot can be adapted for this purpose.

Several vendors have come out with methods for adding a network card to portables. For example, some portables can be ordered with a "docking" unit that allows the user to "plug in" while at work and "plug out" when traveling. Several vendors offer network card attachments for Toshiba and Zenith lap-tops. These attachments give users the flexibility of having a network card for their lap-tops, which weren't originally designed to connect to a network.

Backup Devices

One of the most important pieces of hardware that you'll buy will be the backup device(s) used within your network. BACK UP YOUR FILE SERVERS. IF IT FEELS LIKE OVERKILL, YOU ARE PROBABLY DOING THE RIGHT AMOUNT. Check the backups and make sure they're working correctly. And keep backups off-site to ensure that they're safe.

Most of the proprietary servers come with a built-in tape backup system designed to work with the network file server. For PCs that are brought into service as a file server, a number of options should be evaluated in terms of cost and capability:

Low-Capacity Tape Drives: These tape drives are very reliable, easy to install and use, and priced lower in comparison to the newer high-capacity drives.

High-Capacity Tape Drives: These high-technology tape drives offer a lot of backup storage (2.2 gigabytes per tape). They use a process known as helical scanning to write much more information on the tape.

Such devices are more expensive, but are very fast and reliable; they hold a huge amount of data on a standard 8mm tape, which is significantly cheaper than the tapes used by the low-capacity drives.

Depending on how much and how often you need to back up, you might want to use a combination of both high- and low-capacity devices to ensure your data is safe. High-capacity tapes are ideal for off-site storage since they take up less space and they hold much more information.

Optical Storage: Many companies now offer optical drives (CD-ROM) that can hold a lot of information (800MB per platter) at reasonable prices. I have used these drives as an archival backup device, taking strategic "snapshots" of critical data at month end, year end and other critical times. Because the platters are unerasable, the data are protected.

These devices are slow in comparison to regular hard disks. Because the 800MB platters are more expensive than tapes, they should not be used to back up data that are changing all the time.

Bridges and Routers

Bridges and routers can perform several important tasks in larger networks. By installing a bridge at a strategic point in an EtherNet network, two physical networks are created while maintaining one large logical network. The bridge only forwards network packets to the other network when necessary.

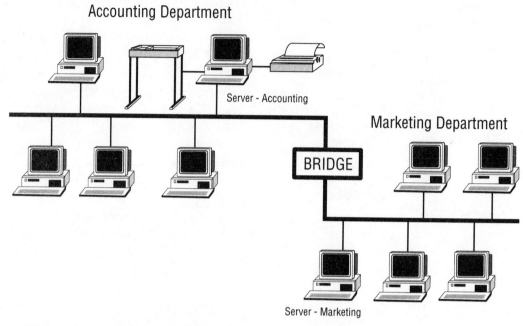

Figure 8.2   Bridging the gap: two networks in one.

The differences between bridges and routers have started to fade lately. Originally, routers were slower, but allowed greater security because they could look deep inside the network transmission packet and screen unwanted packets. Routers could handle only one type of network protocol (i.e., TCP/IP), and would ignore others. A fairly recent innovation, called a "Brouter," combines the functionality of the bridge and the router; it has extensive packet examination but at higher speeds than traditional routers.

If none of this makes sense, get your vendor to explain it, or check one of the books listed in the bibliography for a more detailed discussion. They are very simple in operation, but harder to explain on paper.

Bridges and routers can enhance security between networks by not allowing access to certain portions of the network except by pre-authorized devices.

Remote bridges and routers can turn a LAN into a WAN (Wide Area Network). A bridge is installed on each LAN that is to be connected, and a link is established between the bridges, typically using high-capacity telephone circuits such as a 56KB circuit or a T1 circuit (1.5MB/second capacity).

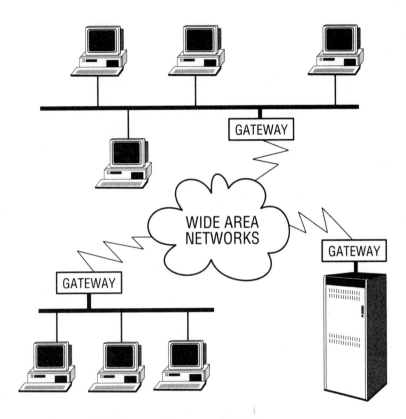

Figure 8.3   Crossing the bridge: LAN turned WAN.

Network Gateways

Network gateways can extend the reach of your LAN as well. With the proper software and sometimes hardware, your network can be attached to a corporate mainframe or minicomputer, national and international packet-switched networks using X.25, or public mail systems like MCI. Many more products are being developed that promise to integrate the LAN with additional devices within the organization and around the world.

Software

Network Operating Systems

The Network Operating System (NOS) is the heart of the network. This is the software that allows all the basic functions of the LAN to happen. Choosing the right NOS for your organization now can eliminate future problems. Going with the market-leading NOS ensures that you'll be in an arena where there is plenty of help and experience available, which is what I would recommend for first-time LAN purchasers. The two network market leaders are Novell and 3Com, whose combined sales currently make up more than 80 percent of all PC NOS products. Below is a summary of their products.

NetWare

NetWare by Novell is currently the undisputed leader in the LAN software market, with estimated market share ranging from 50 percent to 75 percent, depending upon which market research you believe. NetWare (which comes in several different "flavors"—ELS, SFT and Advanced) runs on a variety of networking topologies (ARCNET, EtherNet, Token Ring) and hardware, making it the most versatile as well.

Pros

Most widely used. With its extremely large market share and installed base, all the items discussed in Chapter 6 apply to Novell's software. With its level of testing, follow-on market, widespread support and familiarity, this product is hard to beat.

Fast file system. Performance is generally better with a Novell system due to some proprietary software built into the NOS that manages files and directories on the hard disk.

Many types of networks supported. Novell's software will run on many types of hardware and cabling. Recently announced products include NetWare 386 and NetWare for Unix. So I expect that this widespread support will continue.

Auxiliary products/utilities. Because of the large installed base, a large number of follow-on software and hardware products have been designed specifically for use with Novell's software.

Cons

Proprietary file system. Novell uses its own file system to speed up performance, which makes it difficult to work with. A workstation cannot simply become a DOS workstation, and DOS utilities such as Norton's Disk Utilities will not work to recover files or to reorganize the disk.

Entire solution not available. Some companies want equipment from one vendor. Novell has been extricating itself from the hardware business, concentrating on making more and better software.

3+ and 3+Open

3+ and 3+Open are made by 3Com, which is usually ranked second in terms of the LAN marketplace, with an estimated 9 percent to 20 percent of the market. 3Com makes a lot of its revenue selling network hardware—network cards, network servers, a line of diskless workstations and other network necessities. 3+ and 3+Open are its two major operating system products. 3+ is a mature DOS-based operating system, and 3+Open is the company's OS/2 product, developed in conjunction with Microsoft.

Pros

Strong Macintosh support. The 3+ Mac product allows the Macintosh to use many of the network services available to PC users, such as shared directories, printer services and electronic mail. E-mail is very important, since it integrates Mac users with the rest of the company for communications exchange.

Central name service. 3Com uses the concept of a single name service for the entire network, allowing users access to all the other file servers without being registered (if they're allowed, of course). This can cut down on administrative work in large networks.

Cons

Doesn't support ARCNET.

File system is slower than Novell's proprietary system.

Security isn't as strong as Novell's (directory versus file security).

Less third-party software available.

Network Utilities Software

As with stand-alone PCs, utility software can be purchased for your LAN that's designed to fill in the gaps left by the NOS makers. Utility software sometimes adds new functions; other times it makes a difficult function easy. Some common network utility software categories are as follows:

Menu Software: These are software packages that allow the network administrator to build friendly shells that assist the nontechnical user in interacting with the network. Not only does this save time and eliminate complexity, but it can be a good security device. An example of this type of product is the Saber Menu System from Saber Software (Dallas, TX).

Performance Monitoring: This type of software gives you reports and on-line information about the usage and capacity of your network. Areas such as traffic, number of users and numerous other items can be tracked with tools such as LAN Probe.

Audit Trails: The LanTrail package from LAN Services (New York, NY) allows the network administrator to monitor access by individual user and by file. For example, a log could be kept of all personnel attempting to access payroll information to ensure that unauthorized access was discouraged. This can be especially helpful in large LANs that have many technically oriented people working on them.

Electronic Mail: For systems that don't come with a built-in electronic mail system, packages such as Network Courier and cc:Mail provide this facility for a broad range of LANs. Additional software can be added to allow these E-mail packages to send mail to the world via public E-mail networks; they can provide a means of hooking unlike networks together for messaging.

User Support: Several packages are available for assisting other network users without being physically present. NetRemote is a package that allows the operator to go across the LAN and either view or take control of any workstations loaded with a small-memory resident program. This allows the LAN administrator a fast way to provide support, especially helpful in network environments where the users are spread far apart or are in multiple buildings. This type of software is also good for training new users.

Workstation Software

Each network operating system vendor typically supplies all the software that needs to be loaded at the workstation. For example, 3Com provides a suite of device drivers that are added to the CONFIG.SYS file of the local PC. When the PC is booted, the drivers allow the PC to communicate with the network card installed in it. The network card in turn passes traffic to the network and interacts with the file server.

Workstation software can consume variable amounts of system memory, depending on how it's configured and the capabilities of the network installed within.

Moving On

In this chapter, we've taken a quick trip through the components that make up a PC network, and we've looked at the major players in the PC network marketplace. There are certainly other vendors in this marketplace that have products. The preceding was not an attempt to fully cover the wide range of available products. When determining what is best for your network, work with the vendors and look at the successful experiences of other companies.

For comparing the various products available, order several of the networking or PC magazines in the bibliography. They provide up-to-date reviews and feature listings on a regular basis.

This market is changing rapidly, and attempting to put a full-featured product comparison in a book just isn't adequate. Different companies are leap-frogging each other with the latest and greatest hardware and software. Networks have increased in capability dramatically since I started working with them. And there's almost no end to what can be done to improve capabilities and services. A particularly good sign is that everything is so modular and inexpensive. For example, if you want to add a fax gateway to your network, it usually entails adding another PC with a special card and software. The unit is stand-alone in terms of its operation, so the impact on your NOS is limited. Many products are being developed that will give the LAN user the choice of many beneficial alternatives.

That's pretty much it for the technical stuff. In the next chapter, we'll start looking at how to purchase your networking solution—how to state your requirements, evaluate potential vendors and organize a project plan. If you're moving ahead with a network solution, this will be a critical area. Make sure you have your information plans and goals in order. They will provide a valuable set of checkpoints as you start looking at alternatives.

9

Purchasing Your Solution and Making It Work

You're now familiar with the various components that make up a LAN, the types of networks available, and whether in fact your company needs one.

If you've implemented one of the less-complex solutions outlined in Chapter 5 and it has solved your problems, congratulations. You've saved a lot of money and work that you might have spent on a more complex system.

However, if you've determined that a full-fledged network is needed, you might as well get started now. The major focus of this chapter is on acquiring the hardware, software and support required for implementation.

Unless you plan to purchase all components and install the networking solution with internal resources, the outside vendor, consultant or systems integrator is very important to your success. How you define what you want to the people responsible for accomplishing all this will spell the difference between success and failure during the implementation.

One thing to remember is that these people work for you—and are responsible for making your organization successful. If you feel that isn't happening during the project, stop, question and correct the situation if necessary. The project that is underway will be around your organization for a long time. Make sure it's done correctly.

Get Your Ducks in a Row

Many organizations rush right to the vendor instead of first taking the time to do a thorough analysis of their goals and needs. Various vendor proposals are laid out on a table, and the one that seems the best is used as the model. Asking a vendor to quote on a solution you don't really understand will not yield an appropriate solution. Remember the phrase "pay now or pay later" as you're finalizing your plan.

If possible, attend seminars and workshops. Many vendors offer seminars as a sales tool; although sometimes less than totally objective, they can provide useful information for comparison shopping.

Many expensive networking seminars are offered around the country that offer three days of lectures and some hands-on practice. In general, these are aimed at the person responsible for installing and maintaining the solution rather than those who are making the decisions.

Computer or network user groups are another source of good information; they can be contacted through the vendors or by checking a local computer newspaper. Because these are hands-on users of the product, they can give you tips on pitfalls, news of upcoming technology, and ways to minimize expenses.

Check the latest issues of networking magazines for the latest developments to be sure that the proposed solutions are not rapidly becoming obsolete. Temper your new-found knowledge with the fact that it takes time for new technical innovations to mature in the marketplace.

Timing Is Critical

If much of your business is seasonal, and the high season is coming up soon, you'll want to consider the timing of your systems acquisition. It may be wiser to schedule the majority of the installation during a relatively quiet period.

This isn't to say a solution cannot be installed during a busy period; it's simply easier to accomplish when you're not under pressure. If the solution must be in place for a particular event (for example, the beginning of a new fiscal year), you'll need to leave sufficient time to cover unexpected delays or setbacks.

Are Your Objectives Clear?

If you've read and followed previous chapters, you should have a clear written statement of your networking objectives. Is the system aimed at solving critical problems or adding strategic capabilities within the organization? How are you going to know when those goals have been accomplished? Do you have a specified amount of time in which to accomplish them? Is management supporting the conversion to an electronic method of accomplishing these functions, and does it share responsibility for the results?

If these questions are unresolved, you'll want to wait until the reasons for proceeding are clear.

The More the Merrier

It's typical to have one or two individuals in an organization who have the best working knowledge of computers and your current information systems. For some companies, this is an outside consultant who's on a retainer basis. Adding a network is an important step that will affect your organization, and it's important to get as much input as possible.

Initially, you should bring as many people as possible into the decision loop, and it should be viewed as a positive exercise. If questions are raised and discussed, it can only help you make a better decision. In the past, solutions typically have been dictated by the few computer-literate people within a company. Ideally, top managers should understand the options and make the final decision. This ensures that all the options get an objective review and that management feels responsible for the decision.

Using a Consultant

If you decide to use an outside consultant for any portion of your networking plans, the following guidelines can provide a framework for your agreement. The first thing to remember is, don't sign a blank check. You should know exactly what you're getting and when you're getting it.

You may assume that by the time you've drafted the contract with all the details spelled out, you won't need the help of a consultant. This may be true, but doing a detailed analysis can pay dividends by helping you make informed decisions and keep costs in line. If you have defined things broadly, the consultant may spend a substantial amount of time researching the detail underlying the generalities, and rightfully want to renegotiate the contract based on things that weren't apparent at the time of the original agreement.

Define Scope and Purpose: The agreement you work out should define what tasks the consultant is to do and the objectives you want to achieve. It's important to state the objectives clearly and to make them as business-oriented as possible.

Milestones and Timetable: The agreement should outline the overall time frame of the project, and detail individual milestones within it as well. The smaller milestones will allow preliminary evaluation of the project rather than waiting until the end to make an assessment.

Fees and Terms: The difference here can be substantial, depending on whether you're working on an hourly basis (with an extra charge for materials) or a fixed-fee contract. A time and materials arrangement is normally used in the definition phase of projects that don't lend themselves to a firm quote, but there should be control points here as well. Results should be cumulative, and if the project is called off or curtailed, the results already achieved should continue to provide benefits. If you use a fixed-cost contract, be sure your contract reflects your expectations.

Standards: Ensure in writing that the consultant is using all possible standard equipment within the project. This will allow another person to take over the project at some point without having to relearn or redo a lot of work. For example, specify a standard database in your contract rather than letting the consultant pick one that is unfamiliar to you.

Internal Responsibility/Reporting: The consultant should have a single point of contact within the company, and all tasks and measurements should flow through that person. This will avoid bureaucratic duplication and delay.

Ownership and Marketing Rights: If the consultant is designing custom programs, the issue of ownership should be broached early on; you should have complete ownership of both source and object code. If the consultant wants ownership, there should be either a discount or future royalties for your organization.

Warranty: Because most computer consulting doesn't carry a standard warranty, be specific in establishing both the time frame and the level of guarantee for the work performed.

Project Acceptance Criteria and Warranty: There should be a statement of what constitutes acceptance on the part of the organization. This protects both parties as the project draws to a close. The clearer and more detailed this is, the easier it is to determine the project completeness.

Confidentiality: This is your business, and any consultant has the opportunity to see a lot of confidential information about the business. The issue of confidentiality should be completely covered in a written section of the agreement; any use of your information for purposes other than fulfilling the contract should be expressly forbidden. Your information is also protected by a growing body of laws and statutes. Several people have been prosecuted successfully for information theft and misuse.

Termination and Ongoing Maintenance: When terms of the contract are settled, any maintenance agreement should be specified. Spelling this out during the initial contract negotiations gives you better leverage than waiting until the project is complete.

Going Through the Process

The process of acquiring a solution can be divided into several distinct steps. Each step can be as simple or as thorough as the organization feels is necessary to meet the goals laid out in the planning stages:

1. Request for proposals

2. Potential vendor screening/review

3. Re-evaluation of objectives

4. Final vendor selection

5. Implementation planning and execution

6. Follow-up and re-evaluation

Request for Proposals

One of the best ways to get information on configuration options is to invite several vendors to bid on your network. Large companies usually prepare a request for proposals (RFP). These documents can be hundreds of pages long and contain a lot of detail.

Unless the project is a very comprehensive one for your company, preparing a huge document will not be necessary or even desirable. A single sheet that lists the critical aspects of the solution you're seriously considering should suffice (see page 144).

If you already know specifics, let the prospective vendors know. If, for example, you're in a subsidiary office of a large company, and other branches use specific hardware and software, there's little point in having people quote on configurations other than the one used by the rest of the company unless you're willing and able to deviate from the standard. Stating your requirements as to budget, time frames, equipment, installation and other items will allow the vendors to bid with greater accuracy.

Many vendors cite horror stories of clients who wanted "the usual," only to be disappointed with the results when they received a network that didn't match their needs or their goals.

Selecting vendors to bid on your business is of critical importance. Going to a discount house for components is fine if your staff has the expertise to put the components together with little or no support. If, on the other hand, you need complete and ongoing support, you may need quotes from a large, full-service reseller or a consultant who can also sell hardware and software in addition to a service contract. If you want to keep your options open and have time to sort through many varied quotes, you'll learn a lot about the components and pricing by inviting bids from several vendors from each group.

Another strategy that's used successfully with vendors is to divide the contract into multiple phases. Perhaps an initial phase can be implemented and evaluated quickly as a success or failure. Based on the performance during this initial phase, the vendor may or may not be awarded the second phase of the implementation. This gives you a sample period to see whether things are going to work out the way you want.

Getting the Word Out

How do you decide which vendors to contact? Although the trusty Yellow Pages can provide a list of potential vendors, your best bet is to talk first to others in your community who've installed networks.

Perhaps the best candidates are vendors who've already demonstrated the ability to successfully install solutions within organizations such as yours. At any rate, you'll need to either target specific vendors or be willing to compare a diverse set of proposals against one another.

Give vendors a reasonable chance to respond, in keeping with the time frame dictated by the size of your project and the complexity of your RFP. Before quoting, many vendors will ask to make a personal visit to obtain additional information about your specific requirements (and the amount of money you have to spend!).

If a vendor's representative does meet with you, be sure that he or she uses the time to learn about your requirements rather than using it to give you the hard sell on a particular solution. The time for selling is later if the vendor proves to be a viable candidate. You can use the visit to learn some new information about your needs, and if necessary send out an addendum to other vendors who will be supplying proposals. This will help ensure that you get an "apples to apples" set of quotes to compare.

Following is an example of a typical itemized request for proposal from a fictitious business organization, XYZ Corporation. This will give you an idea of what should be included when you invite bids from vendors. You can substitute your own specific requirements and expand or simplify the entries.

XYZ Corporation   ■   **1234 XYZ Circle**   ■   **Indianapolis, IN**

REQUEST FOR PROPOSAL/BID

Summary: XYZ Corporation is a rapidly growing publishing business whose specialty is computer books. The company is five years old, with 20 employees. Yearly sales are around $5 million. The company uses individual PCs for all information processing, which consists of accounting, inventory, distribution and a lot of word processing. XYZ is soliciting proposals for a LAN that will tie all the individual PCs together, allowing for greater productivity.

Network Specifications

1. The desired solution will connect 12 stand-alone PCs and 4 existing laser printers, but should be able to handle growth to 25 stations.

2. The central file server should be a 386-based PC (not a proprietary server), with at least 4MB of main memory, 100MB of hard-disk storage and at least a 60MB backup unit.

3. The network operating system should be from one of the top three network software companies and should be aimed at PC networking. No additional non-PC equipment (Apple, Sun, DEC) is anticipated.

4. The amount of available RAM on the network workstations should be 500K or more once the necessary network software is loaded.

5. Network utility software should be quoted for the following:

   ■ Electronic mail (internal, with MCI Mail gateway capability).

   ■ Remote log-in via modem.

   ■ User front-end menu.

   ■ Menu-driven network administration package.

   ■ Printer-sharing on server and selected workstations.

6. EtherNet or Token Ring, coaxial/wiring alternatives.

7. Vendor should be willing to guarantee the installed solution for a minimum of 90 days from the date of installation and provide a separate service quote for an additional 12 months.

Implementation Issues

1. The main implementation must take place during off hours to avoid business disruption. Any preparatory work that can be accomplished without disruption is acceptable during the day.

2. Vendor will provide eight hours of basic network training to two employees at XYZ. The vendor will also give a four-hour class on network usage to all employees, and provide a one-hour follow-up or individual session if requested.

3. Vendor will be responsible for reconfiguring the current dBASE accounting system to run in multi-user mode on three of the network workstations. The data will be moved to the file server for central access. XYZ will provide the necessary database software and ensure that appropriate backups of the data are made before conversion.

4. Vendor will ensure that all applications software runs properly once the network software is loaded on the workstations.

5. Vendor will provide a complete diagram of the entire network, including cabling, servers and workstations.

6. Vendor will install and test network utility software listed in specifications.

7. Vendor will set up each user with an account on the central file server and assign passwords to each person.

8. Vendor must be able to implement the entire solution within 45 days of being awarded the contract.

Quotes

1. Quotes should be written, with each line item priced individually.

2. XYZ Corporation must receive quotes by 1 September, 1990.

3. Vendor should provide two references that have had a similar solution installed by the vendor for at least 90 days.

4. Chosen vendor will be notified by September 15, 1990.

5. Direct any questions to Jill Ballou at XYZ Corporation.

6. XYZ will pay 50 percent of the agreed-upon price on delivery and setup of equipment, the remainder to be paid 30 days after implementation is completed and accepted by both parties.

Potential Vendor Screening and Review

Once you receive quotes from several vendors, you can begin to evaluate them in terms of your needs. In most cases, you'll immediately be able to eliminate some because the quotes reflect what the vendors have rather than what you want.

For example, if you sent out an RFP that specifically requested bids on a 25-node LAN, proposals coming in for a minicomputer can be discarded. The same minicomputer quote might be valid if you had specified "a computing solution for 25 individuals within an organization."

While reviewing RFPs, keep the following items in mind:

- The *format* and *completeness* of the quote is important, for several reasons. If it's obviously a "canned" quote, you probably are not that important to the prospective vendor. If you have difficulty relating your proposal to the vendor's quote, your requirements may not have been understood or the vendor may be attempting to switch you to other products. As you read the vendor's proposal, you should be able to recognize immediately that the particular needs of your organization are being addressed.

- Does the vendor give examples of similar solutions that have been installed successfully? This should be a requirement within your RFP; but even without it, a competent vendor should not be using you to break new ground or gain experience.

- How is the *pricing* broken down? Is it one lump sum at the bottom, or is it broken down into individual components within the quote? Many vendors will quote an overall discount; some will discount items individually; and still others will discount based on category of product (hardware, software, services). Is there sufficient detail for you to determine that you're getting everything you require?

- Are there proprietary hardware or software items listed in the quote? If you mentioned specific items or components, does the vendor categorically comply? If you went to the trouble of specifying them, the vendor should include them, or offer explanations and sufficient detail on any substituted items to allow you to judge the similarities or differences.

- Rely on your instincts. As you read through the various quotes, put a check mark on the ones that you feel most comfortable with in terms of a simple "gut feel" or intuition. The responses you'll feel best about are those in which the vendor has dealt with your problems thoroughly and clearly.

■ Jot down questions for the vendor that will help you compare the various quotes. Make sure you know what the vendor is offering; assume as little as possible. I have dealt with vendors who omitted small items like computer cables in order to keep the quote low, and then charged for them later.

■ If you have complex evaluations that encompass many areas, you may want to prepare a grid for entering summaries of all the quotes you receive, so you can rank them if necessary. You'll need to decide if it would be worthwhile to pursue this level of detail for your organization.

■ Write down the pros and cons of each vendor solution, from your own perspective. For example, if you prefer not to maintain the hardware, the fact that one vendor offers an on-site service contract would be a pro for that vendor. Another vendor not offering this service would receive a con.

■ Rank the various proposals in terms of price. Examine the ones that are higher than you expected. There may be some necessary additional items you hadn't counted on. Examine the low quotes for clues to a potentially less expensive way of accomplishing what you want. However, check to be sure that quotes are not lower because items have been omitted.

Re-evaluation of Objectives

When you have all the quotes in hand, take some time to review and rethink the objectives outlined in your RFP. With some items you may have a clearer idea of what you can accomplish with available technology. On the other hand, items you may have clearly understood in the requirements phase may become less clear in light of the vendors' responses. The vendors may not be able to accomplish a particular item: perhaps the technology or software isn't available, or maybe it's available but not within the budget outlined in the RFP.

By reviewing based on your increasing knowledge of networking and its costs, items can be prioritized by those involved in the decisions. Some companies may opt to stop at this point, which may be the most logical course of action.

SUMMARY GRID

1 = Low (bad)   5 = High (good)

	Vendor 1	Vendor 2	Vendor 3	Vendor 4	Vendor 5
Format	1	5	2	5	3
Completeness	1	4	3	3	3
Covers all requests	1	5	3	2	4
Service	4	2	3	1	4
Warranty	4	1	3	1	4
Price	4	3	3	1	2
Payment terms	1	5	3	1	2
TOTAL	16	25*	20*	14	22*

*Finalists

Note: Some items could be given more weight if they're more important (i.e., price x 3 for scores weighted more by price).

If you find your objectives changing dramatically, you may want to revise your RFP and resubmit it, possibly to the same vendors, or possibly to completely new prospects.

For example, your company may specify three LANS of ten nodes each in distant cities to be joined transparently (all applications including E-mail and order entry) via normal dial-up phone lines using existing 300-baud modems already owned by the organization. This is not a technically feasible set of requirements, and the majority of quotes would point this out. Some vendors, however, might say "no problem" in hopes of selling you an alternative solution when the proposed solution fell apart! Upon learning that the solution you selected isn't viable, your company could revise its requirements by selected isn't viable, your company could revise its requirements by increasing the communications speed between networks or drastically reducing the expectations for interconnections.

Another decision that frequently changes during this phase is that of using all outside services. Vendors will happily quote custom programming and systems administration, typically at the rate of $60 or more per hour. Many organizations look at this and decide that an internal service resource (either part-time or full-time) may be the better approach.

Final Vendor Selection

Once you have a set of quotes that accurately addresses your requirements it's time to decide who will get the business. If you have made a weighted priority grid as previously described, you probably have a clear idea of which vendors come out on top. If not, you'll have to base your decision on a more subjective feeling about the various proposals you've received.

I recommend that you take the top two or three contenders and re-evaluate once more in regard to the various components outlined in the quotes to determine the primary vendor and backup vendors. This may seem tedious, but this is the time to catch mistakes and errors—before hardware and software start rolling in the door.

How much time you spend in the re-evaluation stage will certainly be dictated by your organization's culture. Some companies want decisions to be made in a hurry, even if some prove to be wrong. This usually occurs in high-tech, high-growth companies where solutions are already overdue. Other organizations require meticulous plans, with little room for error.

A key step in choosing a vendor is to obtain references and follow up on them. This is an excellent way to see examples of working solutions that your prospective vendor has installed in situations similar to your own. Specify the type of organization you want to see; if the vendor can't provide several similar to your own, that can be valuable feedback. If a reference seems too good to be true, ask for others. You may have found the perfect vendor, but getting additional references will help to reinforce your opinion. Ask the following questions of the references:

1. How long has the solution been working? (Some vendors will steer you to installations that are so new they have yet to be proven.)

2. Did the vendor do the complete installation?

3. Was the original cost estimate accurate, or were additional costs added as the installation progressed?

4. Did the vendor offer ongoing support? What about a money-back guarantee or a 90-day warranty?

5. What kind of problems have you encountered? How responsive was the vendor?

6. What benefits were realized as a result of the installation? Did they match expectations?

7. Does the organization know of any problems with the vendor?

Once you've selected the primary vendor, you can move toward an agreement. I would recommend the following:

Negotiate Price or Content: You may be able to get further price reductions from the vendor if it means closing the deal. Another approach is to negotiate for the asking price plus additional services such as extended support, free technical assistance and free software upgrades for an extended period of time. Smaller firms will probably be more willing to compromise, since your potential business will represent a larger share of their sales and because their overhead is typically lower.

Determine an Implementation Plan/Payment Schedule: Work with the vendor and agree upon milestones within the project, with clearly defined objectives. Tie the payment schedule to these objectives, and don't pay until they're carried out to your satisfaction.

If you've broken the project into phases, make sure the vendor understands that each phase of business is dependent upon successful completion of the preceding phase.

Write a Letter of Understanding: For all major projects, try to avoid misunderstandings by writing a comprehensive letter of understanding and have the vendor sign it.

My company recently had a dispute over the cabling of a newly constructed area. The cabling company had quoted the cables necessary for 80 percent of the offices. The other 20 percent required additional cables that were not specified in the original quote. The letter of understanding (accepted by the vendor) clearly stated that all offices should be functionally cabled under the quoted amount. This resolved the issue, since the offices weren't functional without the additional cables; the vendor was obliged to provide them free of charge. Clear objectives stated in the letter can avoid or resolve confrontations during implementation.

Don't Burn Your Bridges: Let the other quoting vendors know where they stand and why they weren't selected. If things go badly with the vendor you selected, you may find that you need one of the others. There's also the possibility of future business relationships with these companies.

Implementation Planning and Execution

At this point in the project, you have a vendor, a proposal and great expectations. This is the time to develop a project plan that will assure a smooth installation—not only from a hardware and software standpoint, but also in regard to the people who will use the systems.

In many projects, the emphasis is placed on the technical progress that has been achieved rather than overall improvement of the organization. Installing computers and network cable is certainly a completed technical step, but until those installations result in benefits to the organization, they're a liability.

Your vendor should be able to give you a basic project plan, though it will probably have to be coordinated with the arrival of any equipment ordered and the vendor's training classes. If you're paying a consultant to plan and install your solution, he or she should formulate a customized plan that is geared to your organization's capabilities.

The person within the organization who's responsible for the success of the network should have final sign-off authority on the project plan, to assure that all the loose ends are tied up, including the coordination of "buy-in" or support from other individuals responsible for any separate pieces of the project. A project plan that is unrealistic or ambiguous will have to be redrawn at a later date, so it's important to do a good job in the beginning.

Below is a sample project plan for XYZ's network implementation. It is not intended to be complete to the last detail, but is designed to give the reader an idea of how such a plan might be structured. It assumes the vendor has been chosen and the contract negotiated.

SAMPLE PROJECT PLAN

Objectives

1. Install network server, cables and software.

2. Set up and test all network operating software, utility software, user directories and security.

3. Convert the single-user PC accounting system to a multi-user version.

4. Train end users on how to operate the new system.

Preparation (prior to implementation)

1. Run EtherNet cable to all workstations and test.

2. Load network operating software on server and test.

3. Load utility software on servers and test.

4. Build user accounts and directories.

5. Test backup device on server.

6. Back up and purge hard disks on all workstations.

7. Document all operational daily procedures and software used.

8. Develop and test standard network software disk for workstations.

9. Develop and test user network menu and user procedures.

10. Overview training for network administrator and employees.

11. Develop test and contingency plan for implementation.

12. Schedule live implementation for off-hours after review with management.

13. Fine-tune implementation checklist.

Implementation

1. Complete backups of all data, verified and labeled.

2. Install network card and software in the least important workstation, then test.

3. Install primary network printer and test.

4. Install and test network cards and software on remaining PCs.

5. Install and test remaining printers.

6. Test all utility software (electronic mail, etc.).

7. Verify that all previous applications software still works.

8. Convert accounting data to central file server.

9. Install multi-user database software.

10. Verify full accounting functionality and control totals.

11. Full backup when implementation is complete (3:30 AM?).

12. Short round of silent prayers.

Operation

1. Begin problem log immediately for any problem.

2. Verify with primary users that existing functions are working.

3. Begin hands-on training on new functions (electronic mail, etc.).

4. Debug user procedures for various network functions.

5. Monitor performance, disk space and errors on file server.

6. Get all possible feedback from people using network.

7. Start aggressive backup program for file server.

8. Meet with management and vendor to review acceptance criteria.

9. If everything works, go have a beer or a milkshake. You've earned it!

Project Walk-Through

One of the best ways to review a project plan is to arrange a walk-through. To accomplish this, schedule some quiet time with the people responsible for the project and those who'll be working with the system once it's installed.

This is also the time to get your organizational skeptics involved. Lay out the project plan to everyone, and ask for questions. Explain each step in detail, encouraging people to ask questions about anything they don't understand or contribute any information they can. Feedback from the people responsible for making the system work will help pinpoint potential problems. If you don't know the answer to particular questions, research the issues and meet again to review them. The session should include a structured presentation of the project plan, and a general group discussion.

Contingency Plan

One important item to cover within the project review is what will happen if things don't work. No amount of planning can assure that all will go well; the intelligent project plan will allow for the unforeseen and unpredictable. The answer may be as simple as preserving the old system until the new one is up and running successfully, or continuing to run duplicate systems until all the "bugs" are worked out.

The contingency plan may be more or less complex depending on the problem. For example, what if you run the new inventory system for one week and discover that it has problems balancing the amount of inventory on the shipping dock? You may need to keep the manual card system up-to-date for a while after the switch-over, or develop a comprehensive reconciliation process designed to ensure complete accountability of inventory.

Impact on People

Installing a new system can create a lot of stress within an organization. People can become anxious when the familiar ways of accomplishing things are changed. Some people may feel threatened by the new system, fearing that they'll be replaced, or that methods previously used will be exposed as haphazard.

The project plan should address these issues as well, clearly outlining what the system is to accomplish and the efforts required by all to make this happen. Alleviating the uncertainty can go a long way toward making the solution work.

Impact on Business

The project plan should take the organization's necessary daily activities into account. Running cabling while people are handling customer phone calls can be very disruptive. Taking the accountant's PC apart to install the computer network card on the same day quarterly financial reports are due can create chaos! Backups of all information should be made, so that if worse comes to worst, things can go back to the way they were.

Follow-up and Re-evaluation

Once your system has been working for a period of time (how long depends on your organization), it's time to review how things went and what has been accomplished. Did the project work out the way you wanted? Are the benefits being realized as planned? Were unforeseen benefits realized, making the system even more valuable? Or did excessive, unplanned costs eat into the benefits obtained? How could it have been done differently and better? What can be learned for later phases of automation?

Taking time for review will result in a better understanding of what has been accomplished as well as what did not get finished. Some project "drift" is to be expected; few people can completely predict the end results unless the project is very small and specific in scope. Reviewing how the organization handled change can give good information for later projects: should things have gone faster, or should you have done more planning, training and detailed implementation designing? Is top management satisfied with the results? Can the vendor or external consultant (now that they've been paid) provide constructive feedback on how things could have gone better?

A first project review should take place about 30 days after your solution has been installed—and before you issue final payment to your vendor! That makes it a lot easier to straighten out any glitches or discrepancies you may have discovered.

Moving On

Installing a network or similar solution is fairly straightforward, and once you begin to research your needs, you'll find the same lingo, strategies and solutions popping up, which should give you more confidence. View networking as you do any other big project; stick to these rules and you won't go wrong:

1. Thoroughly research your needs and options.

2. Prepare a request for quotations.

3. Take the time to choose the right vendor.

4. Check your vendor's references before making a final selection.

5. Pay in installments, based upon key performance milestones.

6. Take the time to inform your employees about changes that will affect them.

7. Evaluate 30 days after the network is installed.

It's your system. When all is said and done, the solution and systems you acquire are yours and will affect your organization for years to come. Make sure you're comfortable with them from all aspects—cost, functionality, integration and operation.

Also, be sure you have vendors take the time to explain the meaning of the options so that you understand them and answer any other questions you may have. They'll be leaving; you'll be staying. The sooner they leave, the sooner you're on your own.

In the next chapter, we'll look at keeping your network operating on a daily basis. Early in the implementation process, it may get chaotic, but as the process progresses, it should start to blend into the background for most users. The only time you might start thinking about it is when it breaks. You'll learn how to minimize breakdowns and their impact, as well as looking at events that will occur with most networks—growth and change.

10

Keeping Your Network Operational

Once your LAN is up and working, all you have to do is sit back, compute and watch the benefits roll in, right? Wrong. Keeping a LAN operational takes work, planning and determination. Weeks of effort can be lost when a system is not backed up. A break in a cable can cripple entire segments of the cable, putting key users out of commission for hours if a plan for trouble-shooting isn't in place with people trained to execute it. Once things are working, it becomes even more important to protect your incoming benefits.

Problems will occur. So what else is new? You should build a contingency plan to cover expected problems, one that is well thought out and clearly written, and it should be reviewed by top management. With a proper plan, you'll see that alternative strategies can be developed to keep the network up and running, so that people can continue working while the network is down.

This isn't to say that emergencies will occur every waking minute; your LAN wouldn't be worth the trouble if it were constantly breaking. However, it seems as if Murphy's law is in effect when there are network problems: the main network person went home sick, and you can't find his backup person. Bill thinks he can fix it, but ends up really making a mess. This chapter focuses on the things that may happen and what you can do to be prepared if they do.

Assessing the Problems

Network problems come in all shapes and sizes. If you treat them all with the same priority (everything is an emergency), either you or the people waiting for help may develop ulcers (where is that guy anyway?). When you hear about a problem, quickly assess the impact on the business as a whole. If Marge in accounting calls and says that she must manually link her printer in order to produce checks and statements but everything works fine once she does, you can take your time if there are other more pressing matters. On the other hand, if Bob, the president, uses electronic mail to make decisions and direct the company, and the mail server goes down, a remedy must be found immediately.

The first thing to do is apply common sense, but it's amazing how many people forget to do this with networks. Take a moment to review what you know, what others know, and determine the most likely cause of the problem and decide on a course of corrective action. This will save a lot of time and frustration. Your sense of what is wrong will build over time, especially when problems recur.

Below are some of the most common problems you'll encounter within your organization, and some hints on ways to isolate and correct them.

Cable Outage/Break: This is one of the most common networking problems. When a cable breaks or is taken apart, all hell breaks loose. If your environment is thin EtherNet cabling, all computers on that particular segment will cease to function.

Within my company's network, we frequently run into questions about how to distinguish cabling problems from workstation problems. To find the answer, we take a portable computer equipped with a network card and plug it into the network in place of the questionable computer. If the portable works, the cable can be eliminated (in most cases) as the source of the problem. However, if both the workstation and the portable computer exhibit the same problems, the machine is considered okay, and work can proceed on the cable or some other "upstream" problem.

The best way to locate a break is to first scan for obvious problems, asking people if they've done any moving, plugging or unplugging. If that doesn't turn up any obvious solutions, cut the segment in half by moving the terminator from the end of the segment to the midpoint of the segment. If the break goes away, you know that the break is in the second half of the segment. Repeat the testing with the terminator: move to the three-quarter mark, and so on, until the bad piece of cable is located.

Power Outages: Frequent power losses on an unprotected network can cause havoc. Once the power comes back on, all servers should be checked for proper operation and configuration. Application data should be checked to be sure that no data were lost or corrupted when the file server function was interrupted.

One way to solve this problem is to install an uninterruptible power supply (UPS), which will allow any devices plugged into it to continue operating after the power has gone off. These devices start at $500 and quickly get more expensive. Unless your network must run even with the lights off, you can use a UPS unit for the servers and one workstation. When the power goes off, you'll have a grace period to shut down the network servers to prevent damage to the circuits.

File-Server Incompatibilities: If you have a large network, you may have to take a gradual approach when a new version of the server or workstation software is released. If your resources are limited, it will be difficult to upgrade the entire network at once, so some crossover time will be necessary.

As an interim solution, you could leave some of the servers or workstations on the old software and put some on the new version. If the vendor did the job correctly, this arrangement should work. But if a problem does come up, you should start your trouble-shooting by checking out any recent changes made to the network.

Workstation Software Problems: Another problem that may come up is that individual workstations will start misbehaving or cease working. Again, the first thing to look for is what changed. Has a new version of MS-DOS or OS/2 been installed on the machine? How about new applications software? You can look at the creation date of important system files (CONFIG.SYS and AUTOEXEC.BAT) to see if they've been altered.

Disk Crash or Other Catastrophic Failure: Personal computers have improved steadily over the last few years. Advances in hard-disk technology have made disk drives larger, faster, quieter and more reliable. This gives many people a false sense of security; they're still mechanical devices and they will still fail occasionally.

If this happens, don't panic. Resist the urge to slap a solution together. Take time to think through the options. If you have a contingency plan in place, use it to determine the best course of action. If you have only one file server and it fails, you may be able to reload the data and server software on someone's PC while it's being repaired or replaced. Valuable data may be saved if the disk was not physically damaged, so be careful with the broken unit.

Personnel Turnover: Your network "guru" has just resigned to go to work for the vendor who sold you the network! He assures you that in the two weeks before he leaves he will complete the documentation he's been meaning to do, and thoroughly train his replacement. Your year-end financials are due the week after he leaves. (All kinds of problems developed in last year's closing.) Pre-planning for this type of situation is important. Have a backup person already trained. Make sure documentation is done as you go along rather than after the fact.

Complete Disaster (fire, theft, flood, etc.): You arrive at your office building and notice a large bonfire, a number of firetrucks and people running around in raincoats. Or in another scenario, you open your office door and everything is gone—furniture, computers, your favorite coffee mug. Is this going to be a bad day or what? How do you let your customers know their orders aren't coming? How do you know what orders you had?

These examples sound far-fetched, but they happen and they should be planned for. Keeping a recent backup of all vital information off-site is the only way to completely rebuild your information. It's far easier to assemble the hardware necessary than it is to re-create lost information.

Performance Degradation: If performance drops overnight, look at what has changed. Did someone purchase a multi-user Star Trek game that runs across the network? Maybe a new device has been added. Is anything going on today that wasn't going on yesterday?

In most cases, degradation is a by-product of effective utilization by an increasing number of people. Execution that was originally lightning-fast may take several seconds now that 20 people are using the network. It's inevitable that the more successful your network is, the more degradation will occur.

When degradation starts to become a problem, management needs to get involved to decide what is and is not acceptable performance for the organization. This will vary according to the company's needs. It may be better to accept the new degraded performance levels than to spend a lot of capital to restore the original capacity. But a conscious decision should be made to deal with the problem.

Unexplainable Problems/Glitches: Occasionally, you'll experience a problem with no known origin. The network may go out, some bad data may appear, or any number of things might occur. Find out what you can, but if it's not a crippling problem, make a note of it and get back to business. All problems have a source somewhere, but you have to determine what it's worth to find out. The network may have crashed because someone was welding three floors up. Or someone may have unplugged their cable and then plugged it back in, causing a momentary disruption. (I know of a situation in which a microwave between two buildings went out because someone lowered the blinds in front of the sending unit!)

Preventive Maintenance

What can you do to prevent problems and recover from the ones you can't prevent? Here are some steps that can be taken to anticipate most problems and have solutions in place when they happen.

Planning

1. Be informed about potential problems.
2. Prepare a plan for dealing with them.
3. Keep a record of problems and solutions already encountered.
4. Hold a practice drill if possible.

Things You Can Do

The following are suggestions for preparing to handle the problems that may come up. Some items may not apply to your organization; on the other hand, you may need to go even beyond what is suggested here.

Backups and Archives

A comprehensive backup and archive program will save your network and your data in the event of almost any problem. Think of your network and information as a high-wire act, your backups and archives as the safety net. Can you do without a net, or use a small net? It all depends on how important the information is to your organization.

The major problem with backing up and archiving is that it's boring and it's usually perceived as a menial task. But you really need to insist upon a program of daily, weekly and/or monthly backups, depending upon your needs.

You can almost never do too many backups. While this may take extra time, it's very hard to perform too many backups of your critical information. The technology exists to make this an almost automatic task requiring very little people time, but the responsibility lies with you and with everyone else who uses the network to ensure that all data are backed up correctly.

Use your network for backups. When possible, encourage people using the network resources available to them for computer backup. Possibly you can reserve some disk space for backups, rotating each user on a different day of the week. Purchasing a high-speed network device may be the most cost-effective way to ensure that individuals have the tools necessary to do regular backups. *There is no excuse for not backing up the network server—don't waste your money if you don't plan on performing this vital task.*

Management must get involved. You are the ultimate loser if information is destroyed, therefore management should be active in the control and administration of a backup policy. Periodic audits by someone not responsible for doing the backups will help ensure that they're being done correctly.

Use a layered strategy. Backups are best performed in overlapping layers to cover an occasional faulty backup. For example, an organization could do weekly backups of all file servers, as well as daily incremental backups of all changed files. By using the previous week's incrementals, the network could be restored either through the new weekly backup or the preceding incremental tapes, allowing for a small margin for error.

Test your tapes. The person responsible for restoring a backup should be sure ahead of time that the restore function will work. There's no worse time to discover that you've been making blank backup tapes than when you need the data that were on the disk that just crashed. I experienced this recently: a new employee had answered Yes to a prompt in the backup operation that zeroed the tape before backing up the data. The problem was, there was valid information on the tape; and answering No would have caused the new backup to be appended to the end of the tape. When did we find out? When the server's disk was inadvertently erased! Several days of E-mail were lost—a sobering experience.

Off-site storage is a must. Making backups is important, but storing a set of backups away from your computers is even more vital. What if you're completely backed up and the building burns down or someone steals all your servers and backup tapes? An off-site storage solution can be as simple as using your own home, or as elaborate as a safe deposit box or subterranean vault in another state.

Security

Some security features are built into most networks, and these basic systems can be augmented with more advanced security devices if necessary. In any case, a certain minimum level of security should be maintained for even the smallest organizations.

User Passwords: All leading networks have the ability to assign an individual password to each user. This password is required each time the user "logs on" to the network, usually at boot time for each PC.

Individual users should select unusual passwords (not birthdays or spouses' names). The system administrator can erase or alter forgotten passwords or passwords of employees who've left the organization. Users should be encouraged to enter the password on the keyboard rather than supplying them via a batch file stored on computer; using this method can leave the machine and your network open to anyone who comes along.

Directory Passwords: Once user passwords have been assigned, there should be a password requirement on all important areas of the network's shared mass storage. For example, a separate password should be assigned for each file category (e.g., accounting files and sales order entry files). These passwords should be changed when someone leaves a department or after a certain period of time, usually on a quarterly basis.

File Permission Levels: Many of the leading networks allow security levels on individual files. If this kind of protection is necessary, it should be used to secure access to sensitive information.

For limited access, files can be secured as read-only, allowing many people to read the file, but not to make changes. A master price file would be a good example of this. Other permissions might deny both read and write access. The payroll file is a typical example of such a restricted file.

Dial-in Security: If your system can be accessed from the outside, there are several security measures that can be taken. Modems can be purchased that will validate a user's security code before allowing access to the network level of security. Other modems will validate the user's code and actually call back to establish contact, but only to a predetermined phone number.

Security measures can be carried to the extreme, making everyone's job difficult. The level of security used for your network should match the needs of your organization. Certainly, sensitive government agencies can justify much stronger security than a mail order business. With most organizations, reasonable security levels work well most of the time. However, you must not ignore the possibility that an employee might make a mistake with the files or might deliberately try to mess up your data.

Standardization

Keeping your network devices as uniform as possible will not only make staff training easier; it can also help when problems arise. While this may suggest bureaucracy, shared resources demand some consistency. Here are some examples.

Workstation Batch Files: Keeping the network files required for operation as standard as possible will help with trouble-shooting and upgrades. For example, you might create a special directory for all the files associated with network usage. Batch files within the directory allow the user to perform common network functions from any workstation. Common evolving programs or functions may be stored on a shared network directory to allow for rapid changes.

Naming Conventions: Many things must be identified by names on a network—usually the servers and the directories on the servers. It's important that some convention be used to provide clues to help users recognize them. On one network I know of, there's a server named ASTSERVER1, called that initially because the machine was an AST Premium 386 computer from AST Research. While this may sound perfectly logical, ASTSERVER 1 is now a Compaq 386 due to a hard disk crash! Confusing? You bet. Easy to change? No, because people are accustomed to looking for ASTSERVER 1.

Directories on shared network disk drives should also be mapped out. Having a directory called OURJUNK or GARYCRAP may cause confusion later. Appropriate names could be ORDPROC for the area where order processing software is stored or USER 1, USER 2, etc., for open disk spaces.

Applications Software: We covered applications software in Chapter 6, and the need for using standard software is worth re-emphasizing here. The more uniform the software, the easier it is to have interchangeable parts and machines around the network and to recover from problems. Having a unique set of applications and utilities for each person will defeat this purpose.

Upgrading Network Software

Due to the rapidly evolving technology, network vendors release a substantial number of software upgrades. The following are some brief guidelines on upgrading network stations to new versions of the vendor's software:

Upgrade Only for Improvement: Often, upgrades will have no appreciable effect on your network. Possibly the upgrade involves nothing more than support for the latest laser printer. If your network doesn't have one of those printers, you won't need the upgraded software.

Upgrade During Quiet Periods: Changing things "on the fly" can be dangerous. For the sake of safety, changes should be made during a period of relative quiet in your company. Check with key employees to see when such a change is best for them.

Have a Contingency Plan: Things don't always work the way the instructions read, and a plan for restoring any changed resources to their previous working state is very important. Back up before you make changes, making sure nobody is using the system and that all the data are on the backup. Back up after the installation, if possible, in the event you have to start making emergency changes. Think about all the little things that can go wrong and test them after the installation but before everyone shows up for work.

Test Thoroughly: Once upgrades are installed, testing on most networks involves some praying and waiting to see if things work. If possible, test all critical functions during the upgrade, going back to the previous software if problems arise. This approach can avoid some of the problems created by running with software that is experiencing problems.

Don't Be First: Unless your network cannot proceed without the upgrades, let someone else take the risk for you. Put the upgrades on the shelf for a few weeks, and then check with the vendor to see if any problems have been experienced by others. This approach may save you some extra work.

Documentation and Diagrams

Documentation is another function that nobody seems to enjoy. It's not as important as a meticulous backup policy, but it ranks high on the list of items that should be up-to-date in the event of a problem or impending changes.

Cable/Machine Diagram: Having a diagram that outlines the entire network accurately is invaluable. Some vendors will provide this, but if not, do it on your own. Hand drawings will suffice for a small network, but automated drawings are easier to maintain. A low-end diagramming or sketching package will allow extremely detailed drawing of your network at a reasonable cost.

Listing of All Server Information/Data Locations: Having an accurate listing of the data stored on the servers is very important, not only during an emergency but also for day-to-day reference. Several copies should be maintained. One should be kept by the system administrator, another by top management, and one off-site with the backups.

Backups Location Listing: Key people in the organization should know the locations of the backups and know which backups are which. This information is tedious to keep current, but it's usually worth the extra effort when an emergency occurs.

Emergency Phone Numbers and Service Agreement Information: Ever notice that you can never find this type of information when something bad happens? You might be tripping over it all the time when things are working, but it disappears when trouble appears. Post these prominently in a common area and keep them up-to-date.

Contingency Plan: The more you can anticipate, the better your chances are of recovering quickly. Having a recovery plan that's been thought out during a calm period can help solve anticipated problems faster than making it up as you go along. If people panic in an emergency and do foolish things, a problem can turn into a bona fide disaster.

Record Problems and Solutions: Many problems encountered on a system are recurring problems, related to certain conditions such as power, specific hardware or a number of other items. Keeping good records of the symptoms and solutions will help the next time the same problem or a similar one occurs.

Cross-Training

Don't wait until the guru gives notice; train a junior guru who can at least keep things alive. If things always seem to be in a state of flux and require the mystical services of one person, you may be heading for trouble. Once someone is trained, send the guru on vacation—not too far away. (He or she probably needs it after doing the installation.) Then see how things hold together.

Learn it yourself if you're dependent on it, no matter who you are. If the network you're installing is the lifeline of your business, learn enough to take care of it. I know several company presidents who have insisted on knowing the basic trouble-shooting steps for their organization's network.

Critical Dependence

"Network becomes lifeline of business." You might wake up one day and notice that the network has gone far beyond being a nice thing and has become vital to your business's operation. Unfortunately, this usually occurs when it breaks down. Finding this out ahead of time with a simple test (shut down the network on purpose) can save you time and effort later. Contingency planning, manual systems and backup hardware can be identified if you do a test.

Investment differs depending on how critical the network is. Only the organization can determine the amount of time and money to invest in technology. As the network becomes more critical, the investment level should go up, although it should be proportional to the results it produces for the company.

Resources should be dedicated to ensure an adequate level of service. If you're dependent on the technology, get some dedicated people whose sole job is to make the system work. It will be cheaper in the long run. Pay those people based on the performance of the systems if possible—bonuses if the system always works, no bonuses if the system doesn't produce the desired results.

Natural Expansion

If your network is successful, it will continue to grow. More people within your organization will request access, and new projects will be planned. But watch out for "network mania." A careful approach to adding the network should be taken to avoid adding trivial applications that can actually detract from the critical functions being performed.

Doing a periodic review of what is happening on the network can have very positive benefits. Some functions that looked promising for automation may have shifted back to the old way, while other items may have jumped out as new and different ways of saving time or generating money.

Another item to look at is reports from database applications. Managers may get report-crazy, causing reams of paper to be generated, only to be thrown away without being read, or stacked in a corner to collect dust.

Moving On

This ends our practical overview of networking and what it can do for your business. In the next chapter, we'll look at the future of networks, what your business may be using in two, five or even ten years. If you've decided to move ahead with a network installation, the cumulative experience will benefit your organization greatly as new technology is introduced.

Looking Toward the Future

Predictions

Generally, networks probably will follow the same path that traditional computers have taken, increasing in functionality, decreasing in price, and becoming more a necessity than a strategic advantage. As industry standards emerge, improvements in networking and communications software should happen at a rapid pace. It took 50 years for hardware to progress from ENIAC (one of the first digital computers) to the Intel 486; it will take much less time for networking hardware and software to make comparable advances.

Barring economic or political catastrophe, the entire world should be well connected by 1995, with sophisticated electronic communications established among all technically developed countries. If you should happen to pick up a copy of this book in 1995, many of the developments predicted here may have already happened or been superseded by even better technology. Anyone reading this book in the year 2000 might find it equivalent to reading the 1889 Sears catalog today.

Even in the 12 months that I've been working on the information contained within these pages, many advancements have come about: the 486 chip was announced, Unix gained tremendous support in the business community, new OS/2 software is showing up, scanners are entering the mainstream, and desktop video production is taking its first steps.

From all indications, the PC network will gain tremendously in capabilities, rivaling and replacing systems based on minicomputers and mainframes, especially in systems that are being upgraded. Minis and mainframes will be strategically integrated into the organization's network for extremely high-volume or quantity processing, but the machine on the desktop will reign supreme.

With the advent of standard interfaces such as Microsoft's Presentation Manager, end users finally will be shielded from large parts of the technology. This shielding will allow them to use the tools without having to learn how things work "under the hood." I've been told that automobiles evolved the same way—the first few generations of automobile owners had to be reasonably good mechanics before venturing too far afield.

Research in the hardware area with superconductors and light-based computers may put the power of today's most powerful supercomputers on the desktop. Digital telephone networks will offer the possibility of very high-speed communications (voice, data, video), even from the home, and software will advance at a rapid rate. Innovations in expert systems and programmerless environments will finally mean the realization of that terribly overworked term "user friendly."

Small business may overtake the Fortune 500 in the race toward automation. Due to the high costs, small business has lagged behind the giant corporations in the past. Large companies ($1 billion in sales and higher) today have a huge installed base of equipment and this installed base must be used and amortized. However, small business, with a much smaller installed base, can make rapid shifts to new technology as it becomes commercially viable. Manufacturers are striving to ensure continuing compatibility, which means that software will begin to carry forward through more than a few generations of hardware.

Home computing should also continue to develop over the next few years, as prices plummet and better software and communications capabilities become available. Many people are moving the office to the home, or "telecommuting," as a viable alternative to commuting, traveling and expensive office space. As improved communications options become available, home-computer users can become full members of business and personal networks. When business organizations upgrade with new technology, today's installed base of computers will move into the home environment.

Advanced Technologies Now Available

Several ground-breaking technologies are available now. I consider them advanced because the majority of personal and network users haven't implemented them at this date. There can be substantial benefits from each of these items if they're introduced for sound business reasons.

Hard-Disk Mirroring/Shadowing: If you've ever turned on your computer and received the message "unable to boot—hard-disk failure probable," you understand how important the hard disk is to your continued computing. Being a mechanical device, the disk can wear out much faster than the solid-state components of the computer. A hard-disk failure typically destroys all the data stored in the computer. If you have an adequate backup, there's no problem; you buy a new disk, reload your programs and data and carry on (although this usually takes hours or days to accomplish).

To help alleviate the disruption caused by such a disaster, some companies offer a way to compensate. One solution involves installing two identical hard disks in a computer; a special disk controller is also installed that will make two copies of all information, one to each disk. This is totally transparent to any applications software, so no other special software is involved. If one disk breaks, the user is notified but can continue to function with the other disk. This is especially important when a computer is set up as a file server for many people. If the disk crashes at 4 o'clock in the afternoon, and the last backup was done the previous night, many people will have to reconstruct lost work.

Advanced CPUs: The first personal computers were amazing in terms of how many things could be accomplished with so little capability. As the years have progressed, microcomputers have increased in power and capability at an amazing rate, with CPU speeds and disk capabilities approaching minicomputer levels. The Intel 486 processor, the latest addition to the family of chips used to build the original IBM PC, has capabilities that stagger the imagination when compared to the original 8086 chip. And other vendors have not been standing still, e.g., workstation computers based on the Motorola 68030 chip and a new generation of RISC chips (standing for Reduced Instruction Set). The race to put a supercomputer under the desk for under $10,000 is on, and the sky's the limit.

When should your business start purchasing these advanced CPUs? If the need is immediate and justified, you should go ahead as soon as they come out, although you might want to dovetail such a purchase with large breakthroughs in speed and capacity.

Faster Networks: EtherNet, one of the original networking standards, has a stated speed of 10 megabits of data per second. When it was invented at Xerox by Robert Metcalfe, 10 megabits seemed like an astronomical amount. Since that time, the advanced capabilities of equipment to communicate has dwarfed that figure.

One technology designed to allow for larger network throughput is called FDDI, which is based on a fiber-optic network running at speeds of 100 megabits per second—ten times the speed of EtherNet. It's rumored that a network is being developed that can handle a one-gigabit throughput rate (1000 megabits per second)—the theoretical limit of fiber-optic media. This is the equivalent of building "superhighways" for data; existing networks (the "country roads") will be integrated into this structure, via "off-ramps" and devices that convert the high-speed signals to the slower speeds required by network nodes.

Technologies on the Way

Hardware

Speed: Computers will get much faster in a very short period of time. So what can you do to avoid obsolescence? Purchase in the mainstream; make the switch to new technology as soon as it becomes stable and accepted; and by all means choose machines that can run multiple operating systems. Avoid proprietary hardware unless no standard alternatives exist. Networks should allow older machines access to newer generation capabilities, providing a portfolio of technology. Developing a current standard within the company with a future plan built in will also help.

Mass Storage Space: The wide-open spaces are coming quickly, with larger-capacity, small-footprint disk drives—1GB is available now and larger ones are on the way. These devices allow much more information to be stored on a single computer or network. Alternatives will proliferate; high-capacity, inexpensive optical disks may become the preferred mode for archives and backups. Solid-state, or electronic, disks are starting to emerge as the 1-megabit chip moves into production; this market should explode when the 4-megabit and 16-megabit chips can be mass produced. These disks are more reliable and many times faster than their mechanical counterparts.

Initially, they'll be used for critical storage, but they should move into the mainstream very quickly. A new generation of the current helical-scan tape drives promises 5-plus GB of storage on an $8 tape. Floppy disks won't go away, but they'll get smaller and capacity will increase: one company recently introduced a line of floppy disks that would hold more then 10MB each!

Very large storage systems will become available, such as the one from Epoch Systems (Marlborough, MA). This subsystem is tiered—it can hold over 200GB (200,000MB) on a combination of traditional hard disks, optical disk and high-density tape, with software that shields the user from knowing which device holds the desired information.

More Variations: Due to the advances with smaller and faster devices, you might find an MS-DOS computer almost anywhere— running your alarm system, your sprinkler system, who knows? Watches have already been released with the capability to hold hundreds of names and phone numbers and to upload and download to a PC. If you extend this idea by several orders of magnitude, what do you get? A Sony Walkstation with an 80486 chip, voice input, visually projected screen and linkage to the rest of the world (all fitting in your jacket pocket)! The fast-paced executive of 1993 may never be out of touch, regardless of where he or she is (a chilling thought for all concerned).

Input and Output Devices (scanners, speech and video): Many new ways of getting information into and out of computers are coming into play. Scanners are moving into the mainstream, some with optical character recognition (OCR) capabilities that can translate a wide variety of fonts accurately, and others that can scan an image in great detail. Images may also be brought in from previously untapped sources—your television, camcorder, camera and VCR— allowing many devices to be hooked together in your home or office. On the output side, color printers are becoming available that produce high-quality color output. High-speed laser printers are providing resolutions that rival typesetting machines at affordable prices. The computer screen may be replaced with a device that projects the picture in front of the user, with no screen necessary.

Software

Since microcomputers were invented, software has been the bottleneck to advances in total user satisfaction. As I was writing this book, the 386 from Intel was rapidly becoming the hardware platform of choice, yet the current software is barely taking advantage of the 286 architecture.

Consistency: I think software is finally going to be consistent and easy to understand. With the number of standards currently slugging it out for a dominant role on the desktop, huge amounts of research and development money are being spent by leading companies. To the average user, most of the interfaces will look the same—graphical, icon-driven, uniform across applications. Whether it's OS/2 Presentation Manager, OpenLook from Sun, X-Windows from MIT, or any other graphical user interface (GUI) products, the user will benefit from these simplified interfaces.

Ease of Use: Like the companies developing interface products, applications developers are building increased capability for the end user. Imagine a truly revolutionary accounting system that would come loaded with all the generally accepted accounting principles (GAAP) and be able to explain to the novice user what a debit or a credit is. You would be able to type in (or tell the computer), "I bought some pens from 7-Eleven on 9/29/92 and paid $11.00 cash for them." Better yet, the 7-Eleven computer/cash register would notify your accounting computer for you.

Groupware: Groupware—or software that coordinates the needs, actions, tasks and information of several people at the same time—will become much more sophisticated.

Some primitive systems are available now, but I think as subsequent generations appear, they'll seem as rudimentary as a flint arrowhead compared to a particle-beam weapon. Imagine an interactive conference with six people that includes graphs, video, sound and animation. Or a multi-user project management system that monitors progress by "talking" to all the individuals' computers to get an updated status. Video conferencing and video mail messaging could become a feature built into many groupware products.

Communications: In the past few years, many advances have been made in the communications field. Modem speeds have gone from 300 baud to 2400 baud in a very short time, and modems such as Telebit's 19.2 Trailblazer offer even higher communications speeds over normal phone lines. This trend should continue, with the capabilities rising and prices decreasing. Telephone companies are getting involved with high-speed communications and advanced services. ISDN (Integrated Services Distributed Network) will offer a global network, with high-speed and highly intelligent connections between individual computers. Local networks like FDDI will allow speeds of 100 megabits and higher between locally connected computers. The x.400 electronic mail standard will allow disparate companies to communicate quickly among themselves by electronic means. In addition to providing speed and convenience, the electronic age may, as promised, save a few trees due to a reduced demand for paper!

Applications: Applications are getting smarter, bigger and more capable. While advances in software lag far behind those in the hardware arena, progress is being made faster than ever before. Applications running on the latest versions of OS/2 and Unix will give users increased capabilities and the opportunity to raise their productivity through a common graphical interface. The standard is still to be set on the desktop, and it's the user who will ultimately decide, despite all the activity of standards committees. OS/2 looks like a sure player, due to the huge installed base of MS-DOS machines, but Unix is growing rapidly as well. Unification of both environments under one standard or complementing standards will again benefit the end user as well as the software developer, who must now change programs to fit the unique interface of multiple operating platforms.

Applications are moving toward more object-oriented design. While an entire book could be written about object orientation and its meanings, in simple terms this means that many applications can be run concurrently, receive information from other applications and adjust accordingly without input from the user.

The Final Word

What do the innovations and problems mean for the end user of technology? One thing is clear: it's even more important to create a solid framework of systems and software on which to build. If you choose the correct base-level technology for your organization, adding new technology will be relatively easy. If you pick the wrong technological underpinnings, it will probably be a struggle, and the words "we should have" or "if only we had selected..." will soon be heard in the hallway.

If you start seeing proposals that suggest redoing everything that's already been done, examine them closely. Either a mistake was made with the original solution; the proposal is misdirected; or it may indeed be time to move toward an updated solution. If the previous solution has paid for itself many times over, there should be no distress, since you've gotten the expected benefits and gained invaluable experience for the next round of implementation.

Appendix

Rules of Thumb for Computer Networking

Planning a System

1. Visualize the benefits of networking in your mind—are they really worth the effort and expenditure? Are they achievable? Will they save you money and/or enhance your ability to make a profit?

2. Don't insist that the new system mirror the old system exactly. If the old system is that good, keep it. Conversely, don't try to automate a badly run manual system—new hardware and software upgrades will not straighten out the mess.

3. If eliminating head count is your justification for computer expenditures, you may be disappointed. What will probably happen is that the same number of people will do a much better job.

4. A stepwise, "pay-as-you-go" approach is almost invariably the best way. You get benefits faster, and limit your liability on a bad decision.

5. Technological innovations are valuable to you only in terms of what they can do for the business, not as technical solutions looking for a problem to solve.

6. If you hear the words "no problem" too many times when questioning vendors, start worrying. If there were no problems, the systems wouldn't cost so much.

7. Any project that can't be explained and justified in terms of how it will help the business needs further scrutiny by management and the technical staff.

8. Unless an application is ground-breaking (not a frequent occurrence), someone else out there is using it. Find them and learn from them. Better yet, have your vendors find them for you.

9. Gut feelings have a place in evaluating new solutions. If you don't feel good about the solution after understanding it thoroughly, don't be afraid to think twice.

10. There's a tendency to believe that bigger is better—resist it.

11. Keep in mind that there will be costs with most systems after the initial outlay for hardware and software. If you think it's too expensive at the beginning, you'll really feel bad by the time it's over.

12. See to it that the person who selected the system is the one who implements it. This ensures a sense of responsibility, involvement and continuity throughout the project.

13. Don't expect a manager to implement a system outside of his or her sphere of control; ongoing top-management support is essential for success.

14. Demand excellence from your computer system in the vital areas of your business. Don't accept pat answers about why something can't be done; chances are good that if it's important enough it can be done.

Hardware

1. Don't assume the most expensive equipment is the highest in quality and the most reliable. On the other hand, don't buy the cheapest "to save money." Cheap, marginal-quality components are prone to a high level of failure and are hard to support.

2. If you can swing it, go with generic hardware that can run a wide range of software; for example, Compaq's 386 PC has the flexibility to run MS-DOS, OS/2 and Unix on the same hardware.

3. Don't spend time and money on technical experimentation unless the benefits are clear.

4. It's better to have ten people share a $5,000 printer than for each one of them to have a $500 printer.

5. The people responsible for producing the most important results should have the best hardware, not the executives who use a computer once a week.

6. Allow for breakdowns and shortfalls: hold on to equipment that can be pressed into service to keep critical functions running.

7. Don't wait for severe overload to get more equipment; watch for the early warning signs.

8. Re-evaluate each part of your system when an upgrade or additional equipment is proposed.

Software

1. A "standard" is something that works well, consistently, over a long period of time. dBASE, WordPerfect, Lotus 1-2-3 and AutoCAD are all market leaders in their respective areas. Follow the well-traveled road unless someone else can prove why you shouldn't.

2. Individualism has its place; but using standard applications will pay big dividends in terms of hiring and training.

3. Buy software clones if they have proven to be good alternatives (sometimes even better than the market leaders, e.g., Compaq and FoxBASE) and you don't need to rely heavily on them.

4. Many software packages are replaced with new ones because no one took the time to look thoroughly at the old one. Make sure there are good reasons for a change.

5. To increase productivity, invest in books and hands-on training for the most frequent users of the software.

6. Challenge people to make breakthroughs and produce results that haven't been achieved before (e.g., customer proposals that include illustrations).

7. Return your registration cards to the manufacturer so you can be notified of updates and potential problems.

Training

1. Fit the training to the proper application and usage level; putting everyone from the file clerk to the president in the same room will not get the job done.

2. Present the training in small, uninterrupted increments. Be sure the theory will be reinforced with hands-on practice.

3. Follow up with people about what they learned. Ask for a demonstration, or arrange for the trainee to become the trainer for the next session.

4. Re-train when a new release of the software comes out, and evaluate the benefits of the new release.

Trouble-Shooting

1. Simplicity is the key word for a low-maintenance network.

2. Make sure that more than one person understands all the ins and outs of the network, so that when the "guru" is sick or on vacation, someone else can step in if problems arise.

3. Always have a contingency plan in the event that one part of the network goes out (including the people responsible).

4. Disaster recovery drills are very helpful; pretend a certain device just failed, and go through the motions of finding the trouble.

5. Be cautious about declaring success with your project too soon. Make sure that smooth operation is consistent and sustainable.

Managing Data

1. Assuming you can straighten things out later usually results in an even larger mess than you have now. Before you install your new system, take the opportunity to clean out some of the information "swamps" that have accumulated. Otherwise, the mess will come back to haunt you.

2. Do the research required to make an informed decision about which information you need to keep and which can be thrown out. The system you are putting in will last for years if it's done well.

3. Look at the paper work of competitors, suppliers and companies you admire. How do they manage their data? Are you better or worse? What can you do differently?

4. Look beyond the superficial purpose of your current data. There may be untapped strategic potential uses in the information you already have. Prospect with questions such as "what if . . ." and "give me a list of . . . ."

5. Make sure you know where your critical information is and be sure it's backed up in multiple places. Consider the consequences to your business if the customer list should be lost or destroyed.

Bibliography

Books

Brenner, Aaron. **OS/2 LANs,** LAN Magazine, 12 West 21st Street, New York, NY 10010 (1-800-LIBRARY).

This book gives the reader an in-depth look at advanced networks, including a review of various vendors' product plans.

Durr, Michael. **Networking IBM PCs,** 2nd ed., Que Corporation, 11711 N. College Avenue, Carmel, IN 46032.

This book provides a more in-depth look at networking products available to the end user and technical user.

Libes, Don and Ressler, Sandra. **Life with UNIX: A Guide for Everyone,** Prentice-Hall, Englewood Cliffs, NJ 07632.

This book provides a very useful history, overview and future directions for the Unix operating system, without a lot of technical command examples.

Veljkov, Mark. **MacLans: Local Area Networking with the Macintosh,** Scott, Foresman & Co., 1900 East Lake Avenue, Glenview, IL 60025.

This book explores Macintosh computers in conjunction with PC networks.

Publications

InfoWorld, 1060 Marsh Road, Menlo Park, CA 94025 (800)344-4636, or (800)227-3265 in California.

A weekly paper, **InfoWorld** is noted for its in-depth reviews of competing products.

LAN Magazine, 12 W. 21st Street, New York, NY 10010 (212) 691-8215.

LAN puts a large amount of effort into articles and columns that address the needs of simple and complex organizations. This magazine is a must-buy and must-read for the person responsible for your organization's network solutions.

LAN Technology, M&T Publishing, 501 Galveston Drive, Redwood City, CA 94063 (415)366-3600.

This is another LAN magazine that has sprung up recently, and it provides some very good articles on implementing the various technologies.

PC Magazine, 1 Park Avenue, New York, NY 10016 (212)503-3500.

This magazine, published twice monthly, offers up-to-the-minute coverage of the PC marketplace—new products, product reviews and continuing advice columns. Don't be overwhelmed by the size and complexity; the summaries and publisher's commentary clarify the issues. The ads alone make this periodical worthwhile.

PC Week, 800 Boylston Street, Boston, MA 02199 (615)375-4000.

As the title implies, this is a weekly publication. It's a great way to keep up on the fast-breaking news in the technology arena. A special insert section called "Connect" deals primarily with networking.

Mail Order

The LAN Catalog, Black Box Corporation, P.O. Box 12800, Pittsburgh, PA 15241.

This catalalog lists software, hardware and accessories necessary to keep your network working effectively. It not only offers standard products for sale; it also gives easy-to-read charts and other information about the major network types.

Glossary

A

Applications software—Computer programs designed for specific tasks, such as accounting or inventory.

B

Backup—A duplicate copy of a computer program or data file, to protect against loss or damage to the original.

Bridge—A physical device with software that connects two networks and minimizes traffic between them by forwarding only appropriate packets of information.

Broadcasting—See Bus network.

Bus network—A network in which each node is attached to a central cable. When one node broadcasts information, it's sent to all nodes at the same time. When a receiving node ascertains that the information was received correctly, it sends an acknowledgment to the sending workstation.

C

Caching—A method of speeding up access to frequently used data from the hard disk; the data are stored in electronic buffers for faster access.

Cartridge tape unit—An internal or external backup device for a microcomputer that uses magnetic tape inside a plastic case. These devices typically hold from 40MB to 2.2GB of data.

Central Processing Unit (CPU)—The part of a general-purpose computer that controls interpretation and execution of instructions. A CPU does not include main memory, peripherals or interfaces.

Client/server database model—An emerging specialized type of network database in which the workstation (client) processes most information locally and requests additional information from the central database (server).

Clone—A computer software or hardware product that acts like a leading product but costs much less.

Coaxial cable—A traditional network wiring medium, composed of a metal core with surrounding layers of insulation and grounding material.

D

Data file—A collection of organized related data records. These are being replaced in large systems by databases for improved reliability and access time.

Database Management System (DBMS)—A specialized piece of computer software used to process structured information in various ways. Examples are dBASE III and Oracle's relational database.

Dedicated personal computer—A personal computer reserved for a single function. In a network, this kind of PC functions as a network file server, coordinating information exchange between other PCs in the network and acting as the common storage area.

Diskless workstation—A fully powered personal computer without a floppy- or hard-disk drive, drawing its operating programs and applications software from the hard drive on the server.

Distributed processing—A method of organizing data processing so that both processing and data can be distributed among different machines in one or more locations.

Downloading—The function that enables a communications device to load data from another device or computer to itself, saving the data on a disk or tape.

E

Electronic Document Interchange (EDI)—A common means for intercompany transfer of information. Data such as purchase orders can be sent between companies, speeding the process of ordering materials and cutting administrative costs.

Electronic mail (E-mail)—A system to send messages among users of a computer network; also the programs that support these message transfers.

F

Fiber Distributed Data Interface (FDDI)—A proposed standard for the next generation of high-speed networks, an FDDI is a counter-rotating ring that operates at a speed of 100MB per second, ten times the speed of current EtherNet networks.

Fiber-optic cable—One of the newest media used for networks, composed of slender glass threads surrounded by insulating and cushioning material, that carries network signals at very high speeds.

File-locking—A technique that denies access to data when another person is using it.

File server—A centralized information storage device that can be accessed by the users of a network. This can be a microcomputer, minicomputer or mainframe, depending on the implementation.

Floppy disk—A low-cost, flexible magnetic data disk or diskette, usually either 3 1/2 or 5 1/4 inches in diameter.

G

Gateway—The hardware and software needed to let two different networks communicate with each other.

H

Hard disk—A data recording medium. A continuously rotating magnetic platter that stores information in either sequential or random-access order.

Hybrid system—A mixture of computer network components from various vendors that comprises an operating system.

L

Local area network (LAN)—A computer network spanning a small geographic area (e.g., an office) that allows information and device-sharing at very high speeds and low cost. A LAN is made up of all small computers or a mixture of small and large computers.

M

Mainframe—A very large computer that can handle thousands of on-line users concurrently. An example is an airline reservation system.

Management Information Systems (MIS)—Systems that provide processing and advanced information to users of applications software. Also the department responsible for computer services in large companies.

Microcomputer—Usually a small, single-user computer that in former times was limited in its speed and capacity. Another term for personal computer.

Minicomputer—A general-purpose computer designed to handle many users and applications concurrently; e.g., Digital Equipment's VAX computers, which can handle from 2 to 500 users at once.

Modem—A device that accepts data from a computer and translates the digital signals into the analog voice-frequency telephone carrier wave, and vice versa. Stands for MOdulator/DEModulator.

Multi-tasking—Concurrent handling of many jobs by one CPU. In a network, this usually means that the file server can be used as a local workstation; other tasks are handled in the background.

Multi-user software—Software that's shared among several people in a computer network. Data files are located on the central file server and shared among various users (e.g., electronic mail).

N

Network—Two or more computers connected to each other via electronic means for the purpose of exchanging information or sharing computer equipment.

Network interface card—A circuit board that allows direct connection of a personal computer to a network cable.

Network operating system (NOS)—Software that enables all basic functions of a local area network.

Network utility software—Software that can add new functions to a network operating system or make a difficult function easier. Examples are audit-trail and performance-monitoring packages.

Node—A station, terminal, computer or other device in a computer network.

O

Open systems—The concept of multiple vendors' hardware and software working together without proprietary boundaries.

Operating system—The program that manages the software and hardware environment of a computing system.

Optical disk unit—An auxiliary storage device for a PC that uses platters similar to a stereo's compact disk. These can be write-once, read-many-times (WORM), or erasable.

P

Peer-to-peer network—A network in which each machine can be a resource shared by others on the same network. Instead of using a central file server, this network uses a "superstation"—a workstation with added memory that acts as the server.

Personal computer (PC)—Microcomputer.

Protocol—The formal set of conventions that governs the format and relative timing of message exchange in a communications network. These conventions apply to data format, transmission timing and sequencing, and error handling.

R

Random Access Memory (RAM)—An area of semiconductor memory that can be accessed in a nonsequential manner.

Record-locking—Used mainly in database applications software, this lets a number of people access the same file, but not the same record, of information concurrently.

Ring network—All computers in this type of network are connected with a continuous ring of cable. When data are passed around the ring from one node to another, each node analyzes the data and accepts it or passes it on.

Router—A device similar to a bridge. A router can screen packets more precisely, to ensure security. However, a router usually can't forward packets as fast as a bridge can.

S

Serial transfer unit—Typically a specialized cable and software that plug into two personal computer serial ports and facilitate the exchange of computer files.

Single-tasking operating system—A simple control program that allows only one computer program to be run at a time. An example is MS-DOS, which can't run both Microsoft Word and Lotus software simultaneously.

Single-user software—An application such as word processing, in which one individual operates a computer to produce one specific output at a time.

Software—The instructions that tell the computer hardware (i.e., disk, CPU, keyboard, monitor) what to do and when and how to do it. A computer can't work without software.

Stand-alone personal computer—A personal computer that's not connected to another PC. Information can be exchanged only via floppy-disk transfer or keyboard entry.

Star network—The original network configuration, which uses a device as a hub for all requests. Each device must have a direct path to the hub.

Switch box—A simple sharing device that connects two PCs to one printer. When switched to position A, one computer can use the printer. When the other computer needs the printer, the switch must be moved to position B.

T

Token passing—A mechanism used by a Token Ring network to determine access to the network by the devices on it. An electronic token is passed from workstation to workstation; a device can access the network only when it possesses the token.

Twisted-pair wiring—The use of standard telephone wire to create cables for high-speed networks. Its low cost and easy installation make it a popular LAN wiring medium.

U

Uploading—Sending data from an originating terminal, usually a personal computer, to another computer or terminal.

W

Wide Area Network (WAN)—A computer network in which the nodes are separated by several miles or by thousands of miles. A WAN may be made up of several local area networks (LANs) or a LAN and a remote computer that has the ability to handle many tasks and users simultaneously.

Workstation—Typically, a 32-bit, high-performance computer, running an advanced operating system (e.g., a Sun workstation running Sun Unix and advanced graphical software).

Z

Zero-slot LAN—A local area network that does not require a traditional network card to be installed in the PC. Instead, the serial plot on the existing computer is used as the connector to other computers and printers.

Index

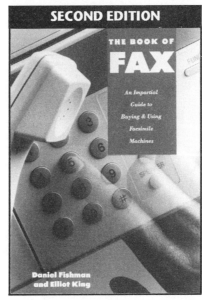

TO ORDER ADDITIONAL COPIES OF
THE COMPUTER NETWORKING BOOK

Please send me _____ additional copies of *The Computer Networking Book* at $19.95 per book. Add $3.60 per book for normal UPS shipping ($1 per book, thereafter); $5 for UPS "two-day" air. North Carolina residents add 5% sales tax. Immediate shipment guaranteed.

Note: 15% discount for purchases of 5-9 books. 20% discount for purchases of 10 or more books. Resellers please call for wholesale discount information.

Name _____ Co. _____

Address (no P.O. Box)_____

City_____ State_____ Zip_____

Daytime telephone_____

_____ Payment enclosed (check or money order; no cash please)

_____ Charge my VISA/MC Acc't # _____

Exp. Date _____ Interbank # _____

Signature _____

**Ventana Press ▪ P.O. Box 2468 ▪ Chapel Hill, NC 27515 ▪ 919/942-0220
FAX 919/942-1140 (Please don't duplicate your fax orders by mail.)**

Please send me _____ additional copies of *The Computer Networking Book* at $19.95 per book. Add $3.60 per book for normal UPS shipping ($1 per book, thereafter); $5 for UPS "two-day" air. North Carolina residents add 5% sales tax. Immediate shipment guaranteed.

Note: 15% discount for purchases of 5-9 books. 20% discount for purchases of 10 or more books. Resellers please call for wholesale discount information.

Name _____ Co. _____

Address (no P.O. Box)_____

City_____ State_____ Zip_____

Daytime telephone_____

_____ Payment enclosed (check or money order; no cash please)

_____ Charge my VISA/MC Acc't # _____

Exp. Date _____ Interbank # _____

Signature _____

**Ventana Press ▪ P.O. Box 2468 ▪ Chapel Hill, NC 27515 ▪ 919/942-0220
FAX 919/942-1140 (Please don't duplicate your fax orders by mail.)**

BUSINESS REPLY MAIL
FIRST CLASS PERMIT #495 CHAPEL HILL, NC

POSTAGE WILL BE PAID BY ADDRESSEE

Ventana Press

P.O. Box 2468

Chapel Hill, NC 27515

BUSINESS REPLY MAIL
FIRST CLASS PERMIT #495 CHAPEL HILL, NC

POSTAGE WILL BE PAID BY ADDRESSEE

Ventana Press

P.O. Box 2468

Chapel Hill, NC 27515

MORE ABOUT VENTANA PRESS BOOKS . . .

If you would like to be added to our mailing list, please complete the card below and indicate your areas of interest. We will keep you up-to-date on new books as they're published.

_____Yes! I'd like to receive more information about Ventana Press books. Please add me to your mailing list.

Name _____

Company _____

Street address (no P.O. box) _____

City _____ State _____ Zip _____

Please check areas of interest below:

_____ AutoCAD   _____ Newsletter publishing

_____ Desktop publishing   _____ Networking

_____ Desktop design   _____ Facsimile

_____ Presentation graphics   _____ Business software

Please return the postage-paid card to Ventana Press, P.O. Box 2468, Chapel Hill, NC 27515, 919/942-0220, FAX 919/942-1140. (Please don't duplicate your fax requests by mail.)